Supporting Information and Communications Technology

MIKE FARMER
and GINA FARMER

David Fulton Publishers
London

David Fulton Publishers
2 Park Square, Milton Park, Abingdon, Oxon OX14 4RN

270 Madison Avenue, New York, NY 10016

First published in Great Britain in 2000 by David Fulton Publishers
Transferred to digital printing

David Fulton Publishers is an imprint of the Taylor & Francis Group, an informa business

British Library Cataloguing in Publication Data
A catalogue record for this book is available from the British Library.

ISBN 1-85346-626-3

Typeset by Elite Typesetting Techniques, Eastleigh, Hampshire

Contents

Preface

For many years the computer has been a necessary evil in the classroom. Teachers and classroom assistants have had to cope with adapting their teaching to the vagaries of the computer. These were usually linked to an array of technical problems, which seem to take an eternity to fix, and software that seemed to ridicule the idea of integrating it into the 'real' teaching of the classroom.

Time has however moved on. Information Technology (IT) is now supported by Information and Communication Technologies (ICT). Computers and other ICT devices have become very reliable and adaptable tools that can be used in a variety of circumstances with ever increasing usefulness. This has been facilitated by improved computer software, the development of networks and the reality of the Internet.

As time moved on, the demands on the teacher and the classroom assistant have increased. The Literacy and Numeracy Strategies, the National curriculum 2000 and the introduction of Early Learning Goals have added new organisation structures to work in the classroom. This is coupled with the continuous need for formalised assessment linked to SAT's , league tables and a variety of different accountability demands that have continued to make the job of working in the classroom more and more challenging. All of these initiatives require precious integration time to successfully introduce and use. All can be supported by ICT. This book focuses on supporting the classroom assistant and teacher in using ICT to deliver these initiatives.

We have produced an up-to-date practical guide that can support classroom assistants in the use of ICT. It provides support in the:

- practical issues linked to using a computer and other ICT equipment in the classroom.
- use of early years software linked to National Curriculum and Early Learning Goals outcomes
- use of ICT in literacy, numeracy, science, art and design and children with special educational needs.
- personal use of ICT, linked to where it can contribute to classroom practice.

It can be used as a stand-alone guide or in conjunction with study on classroom assistant training programmes.

We hope that this book will be an invaluable resource in enabling you to successfully introduce an even bigger resource to the children you will be working with.

Mike and Gina Farmer
Birmingham
June 2000

Chapter 1

Introduction

Computers have been around for a long time but it is only recently that they have really begun to make an impact on school life. The computer in the corner of the classroom has usually been considered an 'add on' and sometimes even a hindrance to teaching and learning. Only during the last few years has the computer really come into its own as an agent for teaching and learning. With the Internet-ready computer, the teacher and children have available to them an infinitely versatile tool that can be used for gathering information on a worldwide basis in addition to being an extremely powerful communication device.

For some time computers have had access to CD-ROMs containing vast amounts of information, but with the Internet-ready computer its potential as a source of information has been magnified beyond imagination. There are literally millions of pages of information available to the user and its growth is exponential. Gone are the days when the only form of communication available to the teacher and children was a runner who carried messages from class to class – in one leap the classroom has moved from the 19th to the 21st century. The Internet-ready computer can be used to send emails, voice messages, pictures and drawings all over the world; at the touch of a button it can be used for video conferencing and live conversations.

The programs that computers use have also undergone considerable development in the last few years. Children can now hear the sounds of the words that they are typing on their word processors and very soon the computer will be presenting words on the screen directly from speech rather than through a keyboard. Programs have also become more interactive, with some independent learning systems (ILS) tracking children's progress and providing them with differentiated learning activities in much the same way that a teacher would operate. Teaching and learning activities are also being offered by the Internet, which may soon become the major source of such resources. What else would give children the opportunity to look at live pictures from a drinking hole in Africa and then switch to live pictures of the South Pole? The computer is now in the position of being able to add new dimensions to the teaching and learning of almost all the subject areas of the school curriculum.

Developments in the use of computers in the classroom are reflected in the early learning goals, National Curriculum for 2000 and the Qualifications and Curriculum Authority (QCA) schemes of work for information and communications technologies (ICT). The main points from these documents are set out below and give a broad foundation for the structure of this book. If you require more details you can usually find a copy of the documentation in school or, if not it is readily available, on the World Wide Web (WWW) at http://www.qca.org.uk

What is the difference between ICT and IT?

Information technology (IT) is to information and communication technologies (ICT) what literacy is to books. You need to have a capability in IT to order to use ICT effectively in your work. IT is the knowledge, skills and understanding needed to use such things as computers, keyboards, ILS systems etc. Without IT knowledge or skills you will not be able to use the WWW to source information or use a word processor to type a report. This book focuses on developing both IT and ICT usage within classrooms.

The early learning goals and ICT

In 1999 the QCA published a framework for the curriculum of the foundation stage which is recognised as being from the age of three to the end of the reception year (QCA 1999). The framework sets out the expectations for children at the end of the foundation stage as a set of early learning goals. The foundation stage curriculum and subsequent learning goals are organised into six areas of learning:

1. personal, social and emotional development;
2. language and literacy;
3. mathematical development;
4. knowledge and understanding of the world;
5. physical development;
6. creative development.

Although the use of computers and other ICT technologies are not explicitly mentioned within these learning areas, it is easy to see the contributions that they could make to many of the areas listed above. For example, computers can:

- be used for imaginative play and working in groups to support personal, social and emotional development;
- be used for listening to and hearing familiar words, and offer the opportunity to use alternative communication systems in language and literacy (other ICT devices can also be useful in this area);

- be used for developing the use of mathematical language and observing numbers and patterns in mathematical development;
- be information sources and aid in finding out about and identifying the uses of everyday technology to facilitate knowledge and understanding of the world;
- help in the development of motor skills and an awareness of safety linked to the handling of equipment in physical development;
- explore colour, patterns and sounds in creative development.

ICT is clearly mentioned when the framework document suggests ways in which the teaching and learning of children with Special Educational Needs and disabilities can be supported. In this area specialist aids and equipment linked to computers can provide valuable support and these are dealt with in more detail in Chapters 4 and 9.

At Key Stage 1 children are set specific attainment targets in ICT against which they should be measured at the end of the key stage (DfEE/QCA 1999). At Level 1 the expectation is that children should be able to:

- explore information from a variety of sources, showing that they know information exists in different forms;
- use ICT to work with text, images and sound to help them share ideas;
- recognise that many everyday devices respond to signals and instructions;
- make choices when using such devices to produce different outcomes;
- talk about their use of ICT.

At Level 2 the expectation is that children should be able to:

- use ICT to organise and classify information and to present their findings;
- enter, save and retrieve their work;
- use ICT to help generate, amend and record their work and share their ideas in different forms, including text, tables, images and sound;
- plan and give instructions to make things happen and describe effects;
- use ICT to explore what happens in real and imaginary situations;
- talk about their experiences both inside and outside school.

At Level 3 the expectation is that children should be able to:

- use ICT to save information and to find and use appropriate stored information, following straightforward lines of enquiry;
- use ICT to generate, develop, organise and present their work;
- share and exchange their ideas with others;

ICT and the National Curriculum for 2000

- use sequences of instructions to control devices and achieve specific outcomes;
- make appropriate choices when using ICT-based models or simulations to help them find things out and solve problems;
- describe their use of ICT and its use outside school.

These are quite ambitious targets and it must be noted that a Level 3 attainment is the highest level of attainment that is expected of a child leaving the Key Stage 1 environment. The majority of the children will be at Levels 1 and 2.

When the role of ICT within the curriculum areas is examined, the interpretation of the statements will be more clearly explained. For example, both Level 2 and Level 3 statements talk about 'giving instructions' and 'using sequences of instructions'. Both of these statements can be linked to the use of a software program called *Logo* or using a floor roamer/turtle in mathematics. Both of these two areas will be dealt with in detail in Chapter 6, *Using ICT to Support Numeracy and Mathematics*.

ICT and schemes of work

In addition to the National Curriculum, QCA have issued guidance on schemes of work (QCA 1998–2000) which schools and teachers may follow in their attempt to meet the requirements of the National Curriculum guidelines. The QCA Schemes of Work documentation includes the following areas at Key Stage 1:

Year 1

Unit 1a An introduction to modelling
In this unit the children are introduced to fantasy worlds and the representation of real worlds on a computer. The objective is to help them understand the differences between the real and the virtual world. This is an important area for the development of learning skills in art and science and is therefore given special consideration in the chapters covering those areas.

Unit 1b Using a word bank
This is linked to the first steps in mastering the word processor and developing familiarity with the computer keyboard. You will find examples of this in Chapter 5, *Using ICT to Support Literacy*.

Unit 1c The information around us
Information is important in all areas of learning, and ICT has offered new approaches to finding information. This unit in the scheme of work focuses on how ICT can be used for communication and searching for information. These issues are tackled in Chapter 5, *Using ICT to Support Literacy* and Chapter 7, *Using ICT to Support Science*.

Unit 1d Labelling and classifying
An important part of the process of finding information is asking the right question and including within that question the correct key words. Almost all information on computers is indexed in some way using key words, so this is an important skill to develop. This is discussed in Chapter 7, *Using ICT to Support Science*.

Unit 1e Representing information graphically
Children will gather their own information and want to analyse it. Graphs are a very powerful analytical tool and this unit is intended to introduce children to the handling of data and linking it to pictograms. You will find examples of data-handling activities in Chapter 6, *Using ICT to Support Numeracy and Mathematics*.

Unit 1f Understanding instructions and making things happen
In this unit children give instructions to make things happen. To achieve this they use a floor turtle or roamer which can be programmed to carry out a sequence of operations. This is looked at in some detail in Chapter 6, *Using ICT to Support Numeracy and Mathematics*.

Year 2

Unit 2a Writing stories: communicating information using text
This unit develops the skills of text editing within the context of creative writing.

Unit 2b Creating pictures: an opportunity to create pictures
Developments in this area begun in the reception and early years are now consolidated. Children learn how to use the variety of tools that are available to them including the brush, flood and spray tools in addition to accessing the work of other artists. This is developed in Chapter 8, *Using ICT to Support Art and Design*.

Unit 2c Finding information
This is where the WWW could be used for the first time in addition to using the CD-ROM. Further information is linked to work in Chapter 7, *Using ICT to Support Science*.

Unit 2d Routes: controlling a floor turtle
In this unit the children learn how to create, test, modify and store instructions to control the movement of a floor turtle. The unit is linked to role of control in the world outside school (see Chapter 6, *Using ICT to Support Numeracy and Mathematics*).

Unit 2e Questions and answers
In this unit children develop their awareness of different types of questions, how they can be asked and how ICT can be used to

answer them using different types of software. They learn that some of the programs they have used so far to present data cannot provide the answers to some specific questions. They begin to realise that programs have limitations and that it is knowledge of the facilities and tools offered that helps them to select the most appropriate tool for a task. This is dealt with in more detail in Chapter 7, *Using ICT to Support Science*.

ICT and working with children

As ICT is part of many aspects of teaching and learning in the primary classroom it is also intimately linked to the realm of classroom support. Classroom assistants cannot avoid having knowledge of IT and working with ICT. The question then arises that if you have been given the responsibility of working with a group of children using the computer, what strategies will you adopt? As a classroom assistant you are likely to be asked to undertake a variety of tasks when working with children including:

- showing children what to do;
- encouraging children to talk about their work;
- offering constructive feedback;
- helping children with their work;
- working with children with special needs;
- working with children for whom English is their second language.

This book offers you support in all of these areas. Each chapter outlines a series of activities in which you may be involved. It is likely that the teacher with whom you are working will originally plan these activities, but the detail of your involvement may be left up to you. The activities all contain guidelines that will help you in the planning and engagement of the part of the activity in which you will be involved. The activities also, where possible, provide help and answers to all the things that could possibly go wrong when you are working with ICT. In areas where it is well known that problems do occur, you are presented with a problem-solving section that attempts to lead you through the solution to the problem.

ICT and your personal use

There is no better way of becoming confident in the use of ICT than to use it yourself for personal tasks. The ins and outs of word processing become easier to understand in the classroom if you have already tackled it – perhaps to complete your course work. Although you will make mistakes, the feeling of achievement in solving a problem area will quickly lead you to being more adventurous, making more mistakes, solving more problems and to a much more enjoyable experience when you come to teach the same skills to a child.

An integral part of teaching and learning is record keeping. The framework document for early learning goals emphasises this point when it describes the role of the practitioner (i.e. the adults who work with children in the settings, whatever their qualifications). A feature of good practice is described as:

- identification of the progress and future learning needs of children through observations which are evaluated, recorded and shared regularly with parents, so that each child's particular needs are met;
- good relationships with feeder and receiving settings and other agencies and carers such as health visitors and childminders. Regular communication, including written records, is used to understand and plan for individual children and to secure children's wellbeing in each of the settings they attend.

Chapter 10 describes how you can set up a record of the children with whom you will be working so that the outcomes listed above can be achieved.

A jargon-free approach to ICT in the classroom

An important requirement of the National Curriculum in all subject areas is that children should use the correct words when talking about objects or ideas. For example, the computer monitor might look like a television but it is not. There are some fundamental differences between the components that make computer monitors and those that make up televisions. Another difficulty is the way that those involved in computers have 'grabbed' words from other areas of the English language and adopted them to describe different aspects of computers and computing. Suddenly you find that a mouse is no longer a small rodent but a funny device that you push over a mat, and the mat is a small piece of plastic rather than something that you would be proud of in your sitting room. To help you come to grips with the language of computing, this handbook emphasises and uses the language that describes computers and computing and includes a glossary to define the computing terms that you are likely to come across in your work.

Further reading

DfEE/QCA (1999) *The National Curriculum*. London: DfEE.
QCA (1999) *Investing in our Future: Early Learning Goals*. London: DfEE.
Between 1998 and 2000 QCA published a series of documents covering different areas of the curriculum, together comprising a Scheme of Work for Key Stages 1 and 2 (published by DfEE, London).

Chapter 2

What Computer?

Probably one of the most daunting things that you will face when you go into your first classroom will be the computer. It is also likely that when you go into your second classroom there will be another computer which will be different from the one in the previous classroom. There is a vast array of different computers and as schools are usually reluctant to dispose of old equipment, the range in a school is probably greater than in any other place where computers might be used.

As a result of a UK government initiative called the National Grid for Learning (NGfL), which in recent years has helped schools to invest in computer equipment, it is likely that you will be using modern computers rather than the older ones. Although this handbook focuses on the more recent additions to the computer world, they still have a lot in common with the older models, so much of what is discussed here will still be applicable to older equipment.

This chapter looks at two aspects of handling and finding your way around computers:

- the computer and the bits and pieces that you will most likely come across in the classroom;
- what you see when you switch the computer on.

Do not panic if there are bits and pieces in your classroom that are not covered in this chapter – probably you will find them in other chapters in which more specialist equipment and software is dealt with.

Finding your way around the computer and its bits and pieces

It is improbable that you will be asked to assemble the computer. This is more likely to be the responsibility of the IT Coordinator or a person who provides technical support to the school. It is however possible for minor difficulties to crop up or you may discover an interest in computers and want to assemble one at home. In both these scenarios a little bit of basic background knowledge may solve the problem very quickly and allow you to get on with the real work of working with the children.

Safety warning
You must never get involved in any operation that involves taking any fixed part of a computer or its peripherals apart. For example, you must not change the fuse in a plug. You may be able to do this at home but within the school this has to be carried out by a specially qualified person.

What is a PC?

A PC – personal computer – is designed to be used by one person at a time. What is commonly called a PC is an IBM-compatible computer. As most of the readers of this book will be using a PC with the *Microsoft Windows* software the main text will focus on this combination. Most computers, whether they be PC, Macintosh, Acorn or Archimedes, are supplied in several parts, designed to operate in similar ways (see Fig. 2.1).

Figure 2.1 The computer (monitor, base unit, mouse, keyboard + printer)

The monitor

The biggest and heaviest component is the monitor (also known as the visual display unit or VDU) so ask for help if you need to lift it. Monitors are getting bigger, the 15-inch screen now being more common than the older 14 inch. The monitor is the screen on which the computer displays its material. Known as an output device, it has a power lead which sometimes has a plug on it for insertion into a normal socket, or alternatively it will have a plug that fits into the back of the computer base unit. In this instance you will find that when you switch the computer off at the end of the day, the monitor automatically switches itself off as well. The other lead from the monitor is the 'signal lead' through which all the information from the computer reaches the monitor. This lead fits into the back of the computer base unit and as there is only one matching socket you do not need to worry about getting it wrong.

The more recent monitors have built-in speakers and a microphone so you might find some more leads which have to be connected to the base unit. The most up-to-date monitors have 'flat screens', take up less room and are easier to handle.

The base unit

Figure 2.2   The back of the base unit

The base unit (Fig. 2.2) is the rectangular box with a series of slots at one end and a lot of strange sockets at the other. This box is the heart of the computer and is sometimes referred to as 'the computer'. In the base unit can be found all the bits and pieces which the computer uses to handle and process the information that it receives from you or the children, including the main storage area known as the 'hard disk'. The base unit will have a socket for a power cable or a built-in power cable that can be plugged directly into a mains socket. Don't plug it in until you have everything connected. You should be able to see the monitor power socket and the signal socket (this will usually have a little white television screen printed near it). The other sockets are for the mouse, the keyboard, the speakers and the printer. After you have attached these items to your computer there will probably still be some sockets that have not been used – these are for attaching other pieces of equipment such as scanners to the computer.

The mouse and keyboard

Figure 2.3   The mouse

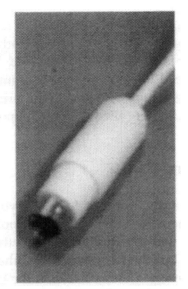

Figure 2.4   The PS/2 connector

The mouse is one of the main input devices which allows you or the children to interact with the computer (see Fig. 2.3). When you move the mouse the movement is mirrored by the movement of a pointer on the monitor's screen. Usually the mouse is attached to the base unit using a connector called a PS/2 connector (see Fig. 2.4). There are different forms of mouse connector so a replacement mouse will not necessarily fit. When attaching the mouse you should be aware that the keyboard connector is usually identical to the normal PS/2 connector. To avoid getting the two mixed up look for the little mouse symbol over the socket. If the mouse ever gets disconnected when the computer is running you will have to switch it off and restart after the mouse has been reconnected. The ball of the mouse can be removed for cleaning. It is normally held in place by a holding ring which can be unscrewed. The mouse ball will then drop out and can be washed in warm soapy water. The rest of the mouse is best cleaned using screen wipes which can also be used on most of the computer equipment.

The other important input device allowing interaction with the computer is the keyboard. Commonly called a QWERTY keyboard, after the arrangement of the first few letters on the keyboard, it dates back to the time of mechanical typewriters and was designed to prevent the metal arms of the typewriter hitting each other. The keyboard connects to the base unit using another PS/2 connection.

In some teaching areas you may find that the mouse and keyboard do not need leads to connect them to the base unit. The connections are 'wireless' and they operate somewhat like the remote control used with television sets.

The printer

Another output device, the printer will have its own power supply and the power lead can be connected to the multiblock to which the computer is also probably connected. The other lead from the printer is connected to the computer base unit and this is the lead through which the computer 'talks' to the printer. The lead from the printer fits into a socket called the parallel port (see Fig. 2.2).

Speakers

Speakers are also output devices. If you have separate speakers these might have their own power supply, which again needs to be plugged into the multiblock, or they might use batteries. The speakers are then connected together and a lead from the main speaker inserted into a socket at the back of the computer. This will probably be the most difficult connection you will have to make as it is hard to see whether to put it into the 'in', 'out' or 'mic' holes. All of these holes are on the sound card of the computer which is the area in the computer that handles recording and broadcasting sounds.

With all of the components of the computer linked together it is important that you try to tidy up the cables as best you can. Hanging cables are dangerous as children can accidentally trip over them. The danger applies not only to the possibility of children hurting themselves but also to the loss of valuable work you might be doing on the computer.

Starting and using the computer

Now that the different bits of the computer have been put together and the cables tidied, it can be switched on.

You switch on and nothing happens. Don't worry about it – this has happened to everyone who has ever used a computer. Try the most obvious first. Check that the main power socket is switched on (where the multiblock plugs into the wall). Check that the multiblock is switched on (some do have switches). Now check that the computer is on. You should see a small light on the front of the base unit. If there is a light then you probably need to switch the monitor on. Still no sign of life – turn off the main power switch, check the plugs and sockets then try again. If this fails you will need to talk to the class teacher or IT Coordinator as there is obviously something more seriously wrong with the computer.

When the computer comes to life you will get a picture on the screen of the monitor (called a 'window'). This may have been set up by the teacher or you might get one of the more usual windows which form the basis of the *Microsoft Windows* operating system. The structure of the window will depend upon several things. The window could be based on the *Apple Mac, Windows 3.1, Windows 95, Windows 98, Windows 2000* or a specially designed window interface structured for the age range of those accessing it, for example school-based *Research Machines* computers may present you with *Window Box*.

You might sometimes be told that *Microsoft Windows* is a GUI, or WIMP, environment:

- GUI stands for Graphical User Interface, which means that objects can be chosen or activated by clicking on their name or on an icon;
- WIMP stands for Windows, Icons, Menus and (mouse) Pointers which are the components that make up the GUI environment.

When you start the computer you may be asked to enter your user name and password. This may be because you are on a network in which individual computers are linked together. Your class teacher or IT Coordinator should have given you a user name and password that will allow you access to the network. Networked computers are able to:

- share resources such as printers;
- share software;
- communicate with each other.

Move the mouse on the mouse mat and see how the arrow in the window moves across the screen. The arrow is called the cursor and this can take a variety of shapes. When the computer starts up it is usually an arrow, when you are using a word processing system it adopts a text cursor shape. When something is starting up and not quite ready, the cursor takes on the shape of an hourglass. In the window on the screen is a series of small pictures called icons. These icons are the doorways to the computer programs stored in the computer on the hard disk. Move the cursor to an icon and double click the left-hand button of the mouse on the icon to start the program. *If nothing happens you might be clicking on the text describing the icon and not on the icon itself.* Make sure that the cursor is over the icon when you click. Another problem is that you might not be double clicking fast enough. Practise double clicking with the left-hand button until the cursor turns into an hourglass and the program starts. If you are left-handed you can set up the mouse to make it more user-friendly. This is achieved by using the **Control Panel** of the computer (see later for information on how to do this).

There is another way to start a program when you are using the *Microsoft Windows 95* or *98* window. On the bottom left-hand corner there is a **Start** button. Move the cursor to **Start** and click the left-hand button once. When a menu panel appears, move the cursor up the panel until it reaches **Programs** (see Fig. 2.5). At this point another panel appears that has a long list of programs on it. Move the cursor over to this panel keeping it within the highlighted area – if you move it out of the highlighted area the menu will disappear and you will have to start the process again. Move the cursor up or

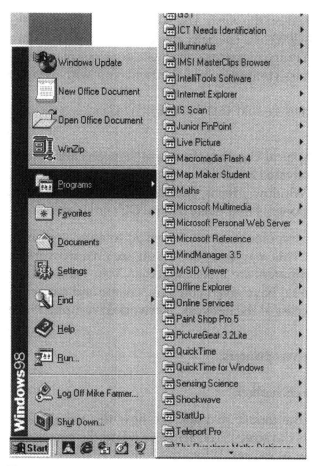

Figure 2.5 Starting a program

down on this new panel until it is resting over the program that you want to start. Now click the left-hand button once. This will start the program.

While you are using the **Start** menu click on the other options to find out what they do. If you want to shut the computer down use the **Shut Down** option. If you want to track down something on the computer then go to **Find**. **Settings** allows you to sort out problems with printers and change most things on the computer through the **Control Panel** option.

Interacting with a program window

Each software package or program that is designed to work with *Microsoft Windows* is displayed in a window. Each of these windows or frames can be made bigger or smaller to suit what you want to see on the screen at any one time. When you start a program it will create its own window which will sit on top of the start up window (see Fig. 2.6).

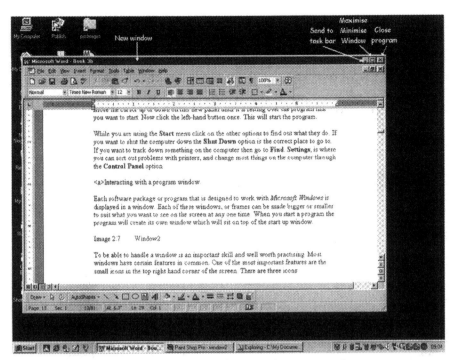

Figure 2.6 A new window and the window controls

To be able to handle a window is an important skill and well worth practising. Most windows have certain features in common, one of the most important being the small icons in the top right-hand corner of the screen. There are three icons and clicking on the '–' sign has a dramatic effect, the window disappears! Look at the bottom bar, the task bar of the main window, and you will see that the window has been packed away neatly on that bar. Click on the title of the program on the task bar and the window is 'magically' restored. This is a particularly useful facility because you can have open any number of different programs and have them all sitting neatly in the task bar until you need them. For example, when you want to include pictures in the text you can run an image-handling program and a word-processing program at the same time.

Clicking on the page symbol has another 'magic' effect – the sign changes from a double page to a single page and the window gets smaller. This is called minimising the window and allows you to have two windows open at the same time in the same computer window, side by side. The windows can be made smaller and larger by moving the cursor over to the window edge. At this point it changes into a two-headed arrow and if you hold the mouse button down and drag you will find that you can move the edge in or out making the window smaller or larger. Clicking on the single page sign maximises the window. Clicking on the cross in the right-hand top corner of the program window closes the program down.

Using scroll bars

If the window contains more information than it can show within its size, scroll bars will appear. If you click the left, right, up or down arrows the information in the window will scroll in that direction. You can also click on the bottom or side bars to move in bigger jumps, or if you click on a bar and hold the mouse button down you can drag the bar to the correct place (see Fig. 2.7).

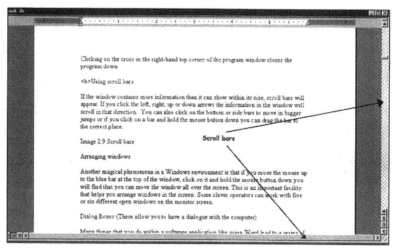

Figure 2.7   Scroll bars

Arranging windows

Another phenomenon in a *Windows* environment is that if you move the mouse up to the blue bar at the top of the window, click on it and hold the mouse button down you will find that you can move the window all over the screen. This is an important facility that helps you arrange windows in the screen. Some clever operators can work with five or six different open windows on the monitor screen.

Dialog boxes

These allow you to have a dialogue with the computer. Many things that you do within a software application such as *Microsoft Word* lead to a series of choices which will often be made using a dialog box. There is no need to worry about them – in most cases it is just a matter of reading the question or statement and clicking the **OK** button. What you will find is that you will not be able to do anything else until you have answered the question or closed the dialog box down by clicking on the **OK** or the cross symbol. The dialog box shown in Figure 2.8 appeared on the screen when the author requested the *Word* program to give the pages a page number.

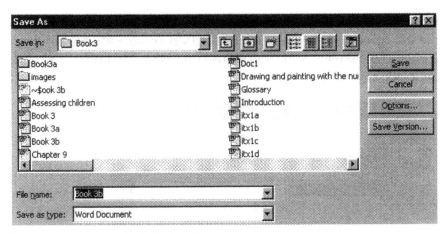

Figure 2.8 A typical dialog box

Using CD-ROMs

Most computers now have CD-ROM or DVD drives. CD-ROMs are 12cm diameter plastic disks which can hold large quantities of information, almost 400 times the information that is held on a typical floppy disk. The information is stored on the back of the disk label so it is important that you do not scratch either the clear plastic side of the disk or the disk label because you may destroy the information that is on the other side of the label. DVD disks hold several thousand times the information on a floppy disk and are at the moment usually only used to store films. In the future we will see them being progressively used as teaching and learning tools linking sound video and text. Your computer will need a special DVD reader to use DVD disks.

The letters ROM in the name of the disk mean Read Only Memory. You can only read from the disk, you cannot save anything on it. The CD-ROM drive is often labelled the **D** drive of a computer. In most cases the CD-ROM is accessible from an icon in the computer window. Slip the CD-ROM into the drive mechanism and double click on the icon that displays the name of the CD-ROM. This will give you access to the index of the CD-ROM and allow you to manoeuvre through the resource.

Installing a new CD-ROM on your computer

Most of the CD-ROMs that you use in the classroom will already be installed so all you should need to do is put the CD-ROM in the CD tray, close it, and click the appropriate icon on the monitor screen. However, you may find that a new CD-ROM has not been installed on the computer in your classroom. In many cases just placing the CD-ROM in the CD drive and closing it can solve this problem. Most modern CD-ROMs will automatically install themselves onto the computer – all you will have to do is click a few **OK** buttons.

Other peripherals linked to the computer

However, if this does not happen automatically, put the CD-ROM in the CD drive and click on the **Start** button at the bottom right-hand corner of the screen. Move the mouse up to the **Run** button and click on it (see Fig. 2.9).

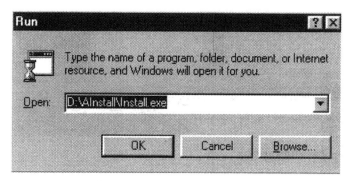

Figure 2.9   The **Run** box

Click on the **Browse** button of the dialog box that appears. At this point you may get an error message which says that the **A** drive is not available. Do not panic, click on **Cancel**. If this does not happen you will get a **Browse** box that probably has **Desktop** in the **Look in** box at the top (see Fig. 2.10). Click on the downward arrow on the right-hand side of this box and choose the **D** or **E** drive or whatever corresponds to your CD-drive. If you are not sure, the computer will quickly inform you if you are wrong. If you get it right, a list of files will appear in the box below the **Look in** box. One of these files will have the word 'setup' or 'install' linked to it. Double click on the appropriate file and you will be on your way.

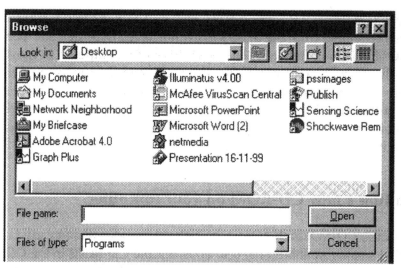

Figure 2.10   The **Browse** box

Setting up the computer for a multimedia CD-ROM

Most CD-ROMs that you will be using will be multimedia and have some sound associated with them. Modern computers have monitors with built-in speakers. Older computers have separate speakers that are usually attached to the back of the base unit. These speakers also need their own power supply, which can be either batteries, or a transformer built into the plug, which is plugged into the mains. Sound levels are controlled directly by the speakers and by the computer itself. The speakers have their own sound level control, either on the speaker or on the monitor. The computer can also control sound levels. Look at the task bar on the bottom right-hand corner of the computer. If there is a small picture of a loudspeaker, clicking on that will give you control over volume levels. If the loudspeaker is not there you will need to click on the **Start** button (bottom left corner), click on **Control Panel**, find the **Multimedia** icon and then click in the box that asks if you would like the volume controls to be displayed (see Fig. 2.11). Once you have completed this, the volume controls will either directly appear, or alternatively appear as a small loudspeaker symbol in the task bar in the bottom right-hand corner of the screen. Click on this icon and the speaker controls will display themselves. At the bottom of the control there is a **Mute** box which is very useful if you want to quickly switch off the sound system of the computer. Sound can also be played through earphones which usually plug into the front of the computer. When using earphones with children you must be careful about hygiene.

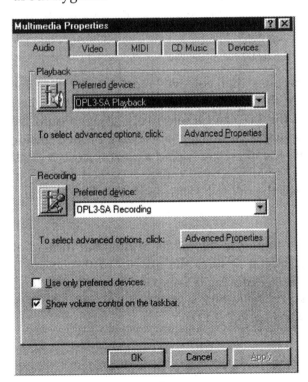

Figure 2.11   Multimedia

The floppy disk

You might wonder why a rigid 3.5 inch square of plastic is called a floppy disk! If you have an old one break it open. Inside you will find a thin floppy disk of plastic on which electronic data can be stored. When the disk is placed in the **A** drive of the computer the metal plate at the front of the disk slides open and a magnetic head in the computer can access the disk's information in a similar way to the head on a tape recorder. Floppy disks will remain an important accessory in schools for some time. The floppy disk is the filing cabinet for all the children's work, and as they are now so cheap there should be no reason why children should not have their own individual set of floppy disks that they can keep with them through their school career as a permanent record of their work in ICT.

Printing

There is a variety of printers that you might meet in the school – some large, some small. They can be grouped into four basic types.

Dot matrix printers

These are a bit like old typewriters in that they use an ink ribbon. The print head of the printer has a series of pins that shoot out when they receive the signal from the computer. The pins make up the shape of the letter, which is then printed. Different letters result in a different set of pins shooting out of the print head. They are robust machines but the quality of the print is not very good and they cannot print in colour.

Ink jet printers

These are probably the ones that you will most frequently come across in your school. In these printers the print head contains tiny nozzles through which the ink can be selectively sprayed onto the paper to form the letter shapes or image that is being printed. Inside each nozzle is a special type of crystal (called a piezoelectric crystal) which changes shape when an electrical charge is passed through it. This shape change causes the ink to be squeezed out of the nozzle.

Bubble jet printers

The bubble jet printer is similar to the ink jet printer, but instead of using the piezoelectric crystal to force the ink out of the nozzle it heats up the ink in the nozzle causing it to expand form a bubble and force its way out of the nozzle. Bubble jet printers use ink cartridges in which the ink is stored (see Fig. 2.12).

Figure 2.12   A bubble jet printer

Laser printers

Laser printers work in the same way as photocopiers. They use powdered ink called a toner which is transferred to the paper after the image to be copied has been invisibly drawn on the paper using a laser. The ink is then melted and adhered to the paper using heat and pressure. Laser printers give a high quality print and are usually quite fast and quiet.

Using the printer

The way in which a printer is used depends upon the type you are using, but there are some general features that apply to most printers and the following section will give you some clues for working and tackling problems in printing. When you want to print something, the command to print has to come from the window of your computer. Look at the program that you are using and you will either see a clearly marked **Print** button or an icon with a picture of a printer on it (see Fig. 2.13). If this is not obvious then go to the **File** button in the top left-hand corner of the window and click on the word **File**. A menu bar will appear and some way down it you will

Figure 2.13   The **Print** icon

see the **Print** command. For some programs you will not have a **Print** or **File** button so you will have to read the instructions for the program to find out how to print. For example, if you are using a *My World* program (see Chapter 4) you will have to press the **Alt** button on the computer to get the menu bar that will give you the print option.

When you click the **Print** option your troubles may be just about to begin! You might be lucky – the computer might be set up to successfully 'talk' to the printer.

Nothing happens when I press the print button. Check that the printer is switched on. If the printer is switched on and it has an **On-line** or **Resume** button, press the button. This ensures that the printer is in communication with the computer. If an error message appears, check that the printer has a supply of paper before calling the teacher or IT Coordinator to help. Try to avoid switching a printer on and off during a printing operation as this will usually result in a load of strange print messages appearing on the paper. If this does happen you will need to stop the printing process.

Stopping printing

When you start printing, a small icon of a printer appears in the bottom right-hand corner of the screen. Move the mouse to the icon and double click the left-hand button. A dialog box appears on the screen plus some text which describes your printing task. Click on the task and it will be highlighted (the background changes to a navy blue colour and the text changes to white). Now click on the **Document** button on the menu bar. Click on **Cancel Printing** and the printing should stop.

Changing the ink cartridge

All printers (with the exception of the laser printer which uses a toner cartridge) use ink in some form or another. For the dot matrix printer the source of ink is usually a tape, somewhat like that used in old typewriters. This is usually just removed and replaced by a whole unit. It is most likely that the printer in your classroom will be a type of bubble jet. These printers have ink cartridges that are fitted into compartments within the printer. For some of the smaller printers you will find that the cartridges are fitted into cartridge holders before being slotted into the printer (see Fig. 2.14). When the printer runs out of ink, stop the printing and this will stop the printer. The printer ink can be replaced without switching the computer off. Most new ink cartridges have a small strip of protective tape over the 'jet' area which should be removed before installing them. When the ink has been replaced all you will need to do is to restart the printing.

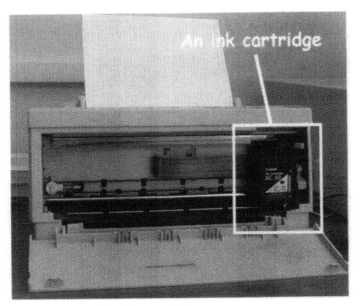

Figure 2.14   An ink cartridge

Scanning

While printers enable you to transfer text and pictures from the computer onto paper, scanners enable the reverse process. Scanners allow both pictures and text to be input (loaded) into a computer therefore a scanner is termed an input device (see Fig. 2.15). The most common type of scanner (which you are likely to use in school) is the flat-bed scanner, but there are alternative types that can be hand-held and there are clever printers that can be changed into a scanner by changing the ink head for a scanning device. The flat-bed scanner is normally attached to the computer through the parallel port socket. This may cause some problems because this is also the socket to which the printer is usually attached. In the latest computers there is another socket/port called a Universal Serial Bus (USB) port that enables chain connection of a number of USB-equipped devices to one port on your computer. For example, a printer and a scanner could both be connected to the socket at the same time.

Assuming you are using the parallel port of the computer, connect the scanner by first switching off the computer and then disconnecting the printer (if one is attached). Connect the scanner to the back of the computer using the parallel port socket. If you have not got a special lead for the scanner it may be possible to use the same lead that you have used for the printer. Plug the scanner in and then switch on both the scanner and the computer. The flat-bed scanner works somewhat like a photocopier. The drawing or text is placed face down on the glass plate and a bright light moves slowly across the picture. The light is reflected onto a bank of mirrors and lenses and is picked up by a light-sensing device and converted into a signal that can be read by the computer.

Figure 2.15 A scanner

The computer must have software that recognises the scanner and allows the two devices to 'talk' to each other. A typical piece of software that can be used for pictures is *Paint Shop Pro* (JASC Software). For recognising text that is scanned, special software called OCR (Optical Character Recognition) is required. The class teacher or IT Coordinator will be able to help you locate and use the software. If you do have problems, Chapter 8 may offer additional support.

The digital camera

An increasingly useful device that is attached to the computer is the digital camera. There is a strong possibility that at some point in the near future your class teacher will find a use for a digital camera. Modern digital cameras have the ability to take small video clips as well as still photographs and it is the ready availability of the photographic record that makes it such a useful teaching and learning tool. The work that the child has completed within a sequenced activity can be immediately recorded and used as instant feedback when discussing cause and effect. Artwork and text can be recorded and displayed in a variety of environments including the Internet. Diary activities take on a new relevance when readily accessible photographs can be quickly incorporated into text.

Digital cameras usually store the pictures they take directly onto a disk or into a in-built memory card. This means that to access the pictures on your computer you have to transfer them. Most cameras have a lead that attaches their memory area to the computer via the serial port of the computer. For some cameras the connection is through the USB port. When the lead is attached the computer software can be used to download, or transfer, the pictures from the camera onto the computer. For more information on using a digital camera see Chapter 7.

Safety and computers

Most health and safety rulings apply only to users who are using the computer for an hour or more at a time; this should therefore not be a real problem at school. It is, however, important that children are made aware of the generally accepted principles of safe working with computers. Unlike many other items of equipment computers do not have dangerous moving parts that threaten the user, but they are electrical devices attached to a 240-volt power supply and should therefore be treated with respect. All cables should be safely out of the way where they cannot be accidentally dislodged. The computer should be properly earthed and the plugs should have the correct fuses. Computers do not use very much power so a 5-amp fuse will be adequate. If the computer is being moved or opened make sure that the power cables are the first to be disconnected and the last to be connected. *As the computer is an item of electrical equipment under no circumstances are you to carry out any form of repair on it.* Repairs to any part of the computer must be carried out by a qualified electrician who can then certify the work.

Water, tea, coffee and soft drinks are materials which conduct electricity so should not be allowed near computers. There should be fire safety equipment, either in the classroom or nearby. Try to make sure that the parts of the computer are arranged sensibly. The keyboard and mouse should be placed where they can be used comfortably. The monitor should be at a suitable distance and angle to avoid straining the neck. The image on the screen should be sharp and clear and in a suitable colour scheme which will not be tiring to the eyes. For children with visual impairments the image should have as high a contrast as possible. Windows in the room pose two problems. The first is that a window behind a screen will give a high contrast in lighting levels that will make it very difficult to work in. Secondly, windows can create reflections on the screen. In both these cases some form of blind should be used on the window at the time of the day/year when the problem becomes apparent.

Adjusting the contrast for pupils with visual impairments

It is possible to adjust the contrast on the screen for pupils with visual impairments. For these children the maximum contrast possible is needed. This is usually achieved by white text on a black background with a Sans Serif typeface i.e. a typeface with no enhancements or curly bits. For example 'a' (Sans Serif) rather than 'a' (Times Roman). To change the contrast of the screen go to the **Start** button in the bottom left-hand corner of the screen. Click and

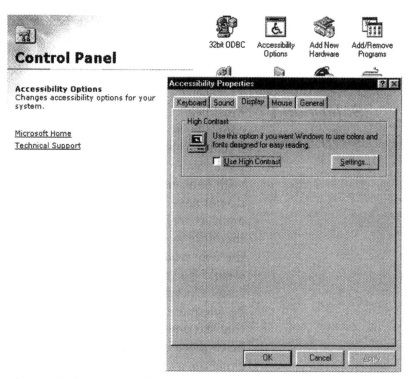

Figure 2.16   Accessibility

go to **Settings**. Move the mouse over to **Control Panel** and click. This brings up a small and crowded window where you will see an icon labelled **Accessibility Properties**. Double click on the icon and then go to **Display**. In the Display area, click in the **High Contrast** box and then click on the **OK** button at the bottom of the **Accessibility Properties** window. You should now get a dramatic change in the colour and text on the monitor (see Fig. 2.16).

Changing the mouse from right-handed to left-handed

It is possible to change the mouse from a right-handed to a left-handed function. To achieve this, move the mouse cursor to the **Start** button in the bottom left-hand corner of the screen. Click on **Settings**. Move the mouse cursor over to **Control Panel** and click. Find the **Mouse** icon and double click on it. This gives you access to an area where you can change several features of the mouse including left/right-hand control, the speed of response and the size and shape of the mouse cursor. When you have made your choice click **OK**.

Further reading   The British Educational Communications and Technology Agency (BECTA) has a downloadable leaflet on health and safety and ICT. The address is http://www.becta.org.uk/technology/ infosheets /html /HandS.html on the WWW.

Chapter 3

Using the Internet

When you link two computers together so that they can 'talk' to each other you create a network. In a normal primary school there might be two networks – one linking the classroom computers and the other linking the administrative computers. These two networks might be then linked to form a larger network, called an Intranet, to allow the administrative computers to 'talk' to the classroom computers and vice versa. This will allow attendance data and notices to be sent over from one network to another but will not allow the class computers access to the financial data of the school (see Fig. 3.1).

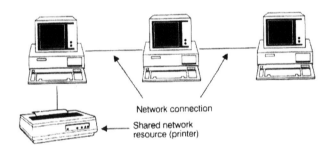

Network connection
Shared network resource (printer)

Figure 3.1   A network

When one network is connected to another (remote) network, and that network is connected to yet another network, it begins to imitate the Internet. The Internet is many millions of networks of computers, throughout the world, permanently linked to each other so that any single computer within any of the networks can 'talk' to another linked computer. This network of computers can be used to support teaching and learning in three ways:

1. as a resource;
2. as a publishing medium;
3. as a tool for discussion and communication.

Before examining these uses, it is important that you know how to connect to, and interact with, the Internet.

Connecting to the Internet

It may be that your school has a permanent connection to the Internet. This is likely to be through a telephone line which is sometimes called an ISDN line. There is nothing special about such a line – it functions in the same way as a normal telephone line but the signal it carries is digital rather than analogue. Analogue signals are like continuous waves of electrical messages travelling through a copper wire, whereas digital signals are the same message split up into lots of little bits before being sent down the same wire. If the school has such a connection then you can start interacting with the Internet soon after switching on the computer.

If your school has not got such a system (the NGfL plans allow for all schools to have one by 2002), you may find that you can only access the Internet using a device called a modem which is attached to your computer and a telephone line. It is likely that this has already been set up for you by the class teacher or the IT Coordinator. If this is the case, the Internet connection is obtained by clicking on an icon (resembling two computers connected to a telephone) on the computer screen (see Fig. 3.2). Clicking on this icon shows a dialog box that asks for a password and a telephone number. The telephone number is the school's Internet Service Provider (ISP). When you click on **Connect**, providing everything is set up correctly, the computer will dial the ISP number and 'talk' to the ISP computer. When the ISP computer has successfully recognised your computer it will give you access to the Internet.

Figure 3.2 The **Connection** icon

The computer tells me that it is not receiving a response from the modem. If this is the case you will need to check all of the connections and make sure that the modem is switched on. In some cases it may be that the computer you are calling is not working so try connecting a little later.

Using the Internet as a resource – the World Wide Web (WWW)

The Internet has been around since the 1960s but was then used solely for communication and data transfer. Then came the revolution. In 1990 a programmer created the first browser, aptly called the World Wide Web browser. Until 1994 the WWW was only text based and had none of the multimedia facilities that we have today. The massive amount of information that is available on the WWW has almost all been accumulated since 1994.

The Internet is a physical resource while the WWW is a virtual resource. The WWW is a collection of accessible multimedia information that is held on computers linked to the Internet. This has created a resource of information that is unbelievably large. Unfortunately, although the WWW does contain useful, accurate and educationally valuable material, it also contains a great deal of trivial, misleading and useless material so you will need to develop your research skills to make sure that the material you access with the children is of the former kind.

But first you need to find the WWW! This is achieved by using a computer program called a browser. Browsers enable individuals to view and access resources on the WWW, very much like you access resources on a CD-ROM. It is the browser that allows you to read what is in the computer that you might be interrogating on the WWW. Your computer will have two browsers:

- *Netscape Communicator;*
- *Microsoft Internet Explorer.*

They are very similar and it is worth trying both before deciding which you are happiest with (see Fig. 3.3). Clicking on the **Browser** icon opens a window which has a menu bar and an address bar or location bar. Underneath these two bars is a rectangular window in which the WWW site that you are accessing will appear. This site is linked to the address that is shown in the address box. For example, if the address is http://www.bbc.co.uk the window will display the opening (home) page of the British Broadcasting Corporation (the BBC). The address that you see in the address box is called a URL (Universal Resource Locator) and it is a unique address for the BBC computer and the information that is stored in it.

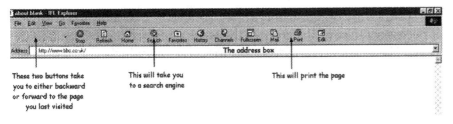

Figure 3.3 *Microsoft Internet Explorer*

Searching the WWW

Like all searching it is best done if you have a reason for the search. A trip to an antique shop or even a supermarket with no idea of what you were there for, or what you were going to purchase, will inevitably end up as a fruitless event. Children will learn more about the topic under study, and about the information communication technologies they are using, if they are clear about the purpose of the enquiry and have specific questions to answer. Information on the WWW is sourced using search engines. These are constantly growing WWW indexes, and no individual search engine has an index to the entire contents of the WWW – each search engine uses different search techniques and builds its index in different ways.

Some use a directory structure (see Chapter 7, Activity 7.3 for a directory structure on a CD-ROM), some use a simple database of key words, while others just specialise in collecting WWW information in specific areas.

When preparing for a search think of more than one word that best describes the subject of your research. When you do get results back be prepared to evaluate what you find. Think about the task before using the search engine. If you know the general category that the information required is related to, it is best to use one of the subject-based search engines like *Yahoo* which can be found at http://www.yahoo.co.uk - *Yahoo*'s website.

Using the Internet as a publishing medium

The great thing about the Internet is that it gives everybody the opportunity to be a publisher! The process of publishing your own web page is not difficult once you have grown confident in using the Internet. If you are new to the Internet it is unlikely that you will be doing much web page publishing, but you may be publishing the children's work in already established galleries on the WWW. In these cases you will find that there is a well-described submission process which asks you to provide the drawing, writing or photograph in an acceptable format (usually as a .JPEG or .GIF file) and link it electronically to the submission box before sending it.

You will first need to take the drawing, writing or photograph to the scanner (or digital camera) and convert it into a digital copy – it is necessary to save the copy of the work as either a .JPEG or .GIF file type. These file types describe the way in which the electronic information that makes up the image is stored and they are the only types of files that can be displayed on the WWW. Make sure that you know where you saved them on the hard disk of the computer. For more information on the handling of images refer to Chapter 8 and for saving files see Chapter 10.

Using the Internet for discussion and communication

If you do not use the Internet for publishing it is likely that you will use it for communication. The most common means of communication using the Internet is electronic mail, or email as it is commonly known. Email is a way of sending messages, data, files or graphics to others on the Internet. There are two ways of sending email: via a dedicated email program or via web-based email. If you are using a dedicated email program you will need to make sure that it is installed on the computer you are using. The installation will probably have to be completed by the IT Coordinator because information on the ISP will have to be entered as well as email addresses and passwords. Once the email program has been set up the sending of an email is a fairly straightforward process (see Fig. 3.4). Click to start the program and select **New Message**. Type in the email address of the person you are sending the email to, e.g. Mike.Farmer@uce.ac.uk, and then some indication of what the email is about before typing in the message. When you have finished the message click on **Send** and as long as the computer is linked to the Internet the email will wing its way to the recipient. If you are not connected, the email will sit in the computer's **Outbox**, until connection. If you receive an email then replying is even simpler. Click on the **Reply** button and a reply form appears with the address of the recipient already included.

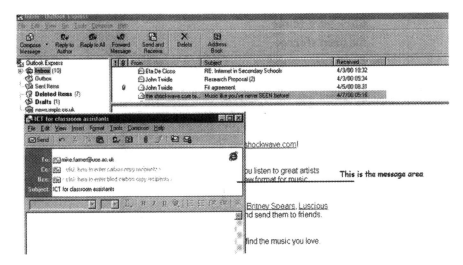

Figure 3.4 A typical email screen

Web-based email via a browser does offer some advantages over dedicated email programs. Users can log on (logging on is the process of gaining access to a site which requires the completion of an on-line form) from almost anywhere and do not have to use their own computer to store email messages since the web-based email provider does this for them. When you send an email it is possible to include with the email attachments of different types. Children love to communicate in a variety of ways and this tremendous facility allows drawings, a sound file or even a video clip to be sent as attachments. The attachment has to be in electronic format and stored somewhere on your computer, either on a floppy disk or on the computer's hard disk. When you have finished composing the message, click on the **Paperclip** icon on the menu bar. A dialog box appears which asks you where the file you want to attach is saved in the computer. This is a complex process, but once completed successfully subsequent use is much easier.

Click on the arrow adjacent to the **Look in** box (see Fig. 3.5). This gives you your basic computer storage areas. If the file is on the floppy disk then click **A**, if it is on the C drive click **C**. Wherever you click you get a further menu in the box below. Can you remember where you stored the file? Double click on a folder and see if you can find it. If you cannot then you will have to go back a level using the **Go back** icon and try again. When you find the file double click on it and it will be copied to your email as an attachment. Knowing where files are is important. It is possible to create your own files in which you can store images and text that will make attachments easier to find. Ask your IT Coordinator for help or alternatively see Chapter 10.

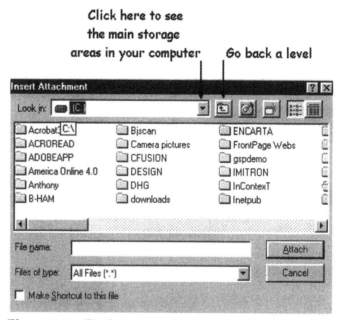

Figure 3.5 Finding your file

Safety and the Internet

The World Wide Web (WWW) is vast and unregulated and therefore concerns quite rightly exist about the availability of offensive material on the Internet. BECTA made the following points in its information sheet:

Children and young people may:

- be exposed to unacceptable materials (pornographic, violent, extremist literature)
- encounter inappropriate messages (harassing, demanding, belligerent contacts)
- arrange contacts and meetings (potential exploitation and physical dangers)
- inadvertently provide personal information while on-line which could be sufficient to put them in danger.

By far the biggest danger to children using the Internet is in chat and newsgroups but there are more hidden threats, for example the commercial aspects of the Internet and children's exposure to marketing. There is an increasing blur on many children's sites between content and advertising, so be careful. The existence of undesirable material is not a valid reason to avoid the Internet. One of the best ways for parents and teachers to become comfortable with a child's Internet access is to become actively involved and use the Internet with the child.

Further reading

De Cicco, Eta, Mike Farmer and Claire Hargrave (1999) *Activities for Using the Internet in Primary Schools*. London: Kogan Page.
BECTA has a series of information sheets to support the safe use of ICT. They can be found at http://www.becta.org.uk/technology/infosheets/html/itadvice.html on the WWW.

Chapter 4

Introducing ICT

Working with children and computers

Throughout this book it is assumed that you will be working with a small group of children, either with the computer or with some other piece of ICT equipment. As quite a few teachers and other adults lack confidence when working with computers, it is doubly important that you plan and familiarise yourself with the ICT activities before working with the children:

- you must know the purpose (outcome) of the activity. Many ICT activities can be used to meet a variety of different outcomes;
- you must try out the activity beforehand. This will enable you to anticipate any problems with the equipment or the software. Make sure that you try out all the steps that the children will go through to achieve the outcomes;
- you will have considered the questions that you are going to ask the children and the vocabulary that you will use. Use the correct ICT terminology wherever possible.

Before you start, consider carefully where to position yourself so that you and the children can use the mouse and the keyboard. In the near future the mouse and the keyboard will be wireless with an infra-red connection instead of wires linking them to the computer. This is unlikely to be the case in your present situation, so the arrangement that you adopt will depend to some extent on the length of the cable. Try sitting on one side of the computer with the keyboard on your lap. This will allow you to face the group and be fully involved in the discussion. Don't worry too much about damaging the keyboard as it is quite a robust piece of equipment. This type of arrangement will:

- ensure that all the children can see what you are doing;
- avoid possible problems linked to the children seeing other groups of children working in the classroom;
- ensure that all the children in the group hear you. This is particularly important if a child in the group has hearing difficulties.

Make sure that the monitor is positioned so that all the children can see it. Try to adjust the height so that small children do not have to look up to see it. Check that there are no reflections from windows or other light sources that make it difficult to see the screen.

Assessment

The programme for baseline assessment (QCA 1999) does not directly imply any assessment of ICT skills. Baseline assessment is directly concerned with:

- language and literacy – focusing on children's developing skills in talking, listening, reading and writing;
- mathematics – focusing on children's understanding of numbers and their use of mathematical language;
- personal and social development – focusing on children's ability to work, play and cooperate with others.

And possibly

- knowledge and understanding of the world – focusing on children's developing knowledge and understanding of their environment, other people and features of the world;
- physical development – focusing on children's developing physical control in moving around, awareness of space and ability to handle a range of objects;
- creative development – focusing on children's imagination and their ability to express their feelings and ideas.

The fact that ICT is not part of this procedure does not mean that it should be ignored in the assessment process and it is likely that your teacher will want some form of monitoring and assessment linked to a child's knowledge and skills in using ICT. Several reasons for doing this were listed in the Birmingham Core Skills Nursery Schools' Project Birmingham City Council (2000). They suggested that monitoring would enable staff to:

- use teaching/group times to ensure a planned progression in introducing hardware, software and the appropriate knowledge, understanding skills and techniques;
- check back at teaching/group times to monitor progression and inform future planning. This should ensure differentiation takes place and knowledge, concepts, skills and techniques are consolidated;
- observe children's use of ICT in relation to other areas of the curriculum;
- observe the children using the computer to ensure equality of access during structured and unstructured sessions;
- ensure equality of opportunity with regard to race, gender and disability;
- observe and record children's use of the computer and level of involvement.

While assessment will enable staff to:

- make a judgement about the development of pupils' IT skills which in turn can be used to inform future planning of ICT activities;
- evaluate the use of ICT within an early years setting;
- recognise broad achievements – social, personal and academic;
- identify weaknesses and strengths.

Assessing the ICT capability of children

In any classroom activity in which we are involved there should be clearly stated outcomes. These outcomes guide the planning of the teaching and learning process and the activities that you will be involved in. In most cases the outcomes will be directly linked to the early learning goals or to the National Curriculum. They will clearly say, for example, for an activity using the *Paint it* (JETSoft) program 'that children will be able to recognise that ICT can be used to create pictures'. This is only one of a large number of outcomes. When we are working with children, we are trying to develop much more than just one outcome. We should also be looking at the children's attitude and approach to learning and asking:

- Do the children enjoy their work at the computer?
- Are all the children equally confident about their computer work?
- Do the girls think they are as good as the boys?
- Are all the children able to operate both hardware and software?
- Are the children well organised?
- Are all the children prepared to persist with a piece of computer work?
- Are the children learning to listen and do they have respect for the contribution of others?
- Can they describe what they are doing?
- Are they considering in advance the possible outcomes of decisions?
- In their conversations do they reveal that they are looking for relationships?

Activity 4.1
An observation
schedule

This is an activity directly linked to your own use of ICT. Create an observation schedule for the children you will be working with using a word-processing program. Use the schedule to record the outcomes of an ICT activity that you will be doing with the children. Chapter 10 provides help in preparing the observation schedule.

This is the second of two activities directly linked to your own ICT capabilities. Using a database, create a table showing how many children in the your class have:

- a computer in their home;
- their own computer;
- a digital television set.

Also find out, if a girl is answering the question, whether she comes from a girls only family or a mixed family. If it is a boy who answers the question, does he come from a boys only family or from a mixed family? Chapter 10 provides help in preparing the database.

*Activity 4.2
Access to
computers at
home by children
in your class*

ICT and gender

Gender issues are important considerations for the classroom and may be particularly important in ICT. There was evidence in the early 1990s that computers were being used more by boys and male teachers than by girls and female teachers. Since then developments in training and computer hardware and software have eased the problem and made computers more accessible to both sexes. There are still some causes for concern and everybody working with children in the classroom should share the responsibility of taking steps to ensure that both sexes have equal opportunities.

Some of the children with whom you will be working will have considerable experience of working with computers. They have probably played with computer games and may even use the family computer at home. For other children the idea that when you move the mouse you get a corresponding movement of an arrow on the screen is utterly alien, and this sequence of cause and effect has to be taught to them.

One of the best ways of introducing cause and effect is to use toys. There are lots of toys on the market that operate on the basis that you do something to them and they then respond. At the top end of the range of cause and effect toys is the sophisticated *Furby* type of doll. There is then a wide range of resources such as programmable toys, musical toys and talking toys. A classic toy is like that shown in Figure 4.1 which vibrates in your hand when switched on and stops when switched off. Finally there is the remote controlled car (Fig. 4.2) which is probably the best link in the chain to the operation of a mouse on the screen.

*Activity 4.3
Toys and ICT*

Figure 4.1 Holding a vibrating toy

Figure 4.2 A remote controlled car

Working with toys with children

The outcome of this activity is that the children will recognise that machines and devices can be controlled. Remember that we are helping children to understand that one action can lead to another action, however remote it may be. It is therefore important to talk to the children about what they are doing to find out if they recognise the consequences of their action. After they have held and handled the toy you can ask them familiarisation questions about it:

- How does it feel?
- What do you think it does?
- What is it made of?

Then ask them about the switch and what they think it does. Ask if there is a child who thinks they could operate the switch and how they will do it. What do they think will happen after the switch is operated? When the object is in action get the children to talk about what it is doing:

- What made it start doing this?
- What is it doing?
- Will it stop on its own?
- How will you be able to stop it?

You can now ask one of the children to switch it off and if necessary repeat the procedure by asking the children how it could be switched on again.

Activity 4.4
An introduction to
modelling

You will probably find a set of programs called *My World* on your computer. The icon for these programs is usually found on the opening start-up window of the classroom computer (see Fig. 4.3). Move the mouse cursor so that it is over the *My World* icon and double click the left-hand mouse button. This should open the program.

I know the My World *program is on the computer but I cannot find it.* This may be because the icon does not appear in the start-up window. Go to the **Start** button on the bottom left-hand corner of the computer window. Click on the **Start** button and then move the mouse up to the top of the list that appears until you get to **Programs** when another menu of programs will appear. Move the mouse cursor across to this list and move it towards the *My World* program. Be careful because if you move the mouse cursor off the list, the list will disappear. When the cursor is on the *My World* title double click and the program will start.

I left the computer alone and everything on the screen disappeared and has been replaced by an image of flying windows (or some other strange animated picture). This is probably because the computer has automatically switched to screen saver mode. There is the danger that if the same image is left on the screen for too long it will leave a 'shadow' of that image permanently on the screen. To avoid this the computer is programmed to replace the fixed image by a moving one after it has been idle for a certain length of time. All you need to do is click any of the keyboard keys or just move the mouse and you will get the working screen back.

Figure 4.3   The *My World* icon

The *My World* programs

The *My World* software programs resemble an on-screen version of 'fuzzy felt' (the technical name for them is a 'framework program'). For many of the *My World* activities there is no wrong or right answer, so the term 'open-ended' is used to describe them. In some cases there may be right answers but it is the teacher and not the computer that gives the feedback to the child. This can be quite useful because from an educational perspective, the 'wrong' answer can sometimes be more important than the 'right' answer. In a busy classroom there is a strong temptation to quickly accept a 'right' answer with little discussion (even though the 'right' answer may have been a guess) while a 'wrong' answer can invariably lead to further questioning in order to find out why that particular answer was given.

When using the *My World* programs an important skill that the children should master is to be able to click and drag. This is the process of clicking on an object, holding the mouse button down, and dragging the object across the screen. The early years programs used in this exercise do however use a simpler technique. The children click the mouse on an object then move the object by moving the mouse. They do not have to continue to hold the mouse button down. When they want to release the object they click the mouse once more.

One of the features of many *My World* screens ('screens' is the term used to describe each individual *My World* program) is a dustbin (see Fig. 4.4). If you click and drag the objects on the screen over to the **Dustbin**, let go, and then click on the **Dustbin** the object will disappear. As a skill development exercise this could be quite good fun for the children. They can then print out a blank screen before starting again and carrying out the activity. Another feature is the text facility. When you click on the **Text** icon a dialog box appears that invites you to type in a word or phrase. Do this and click **OK** and the text appears on the screen where it can be clicked and dragged like any other object.

Figure 4.4
The *My World*
Dustbin icon

Yet another feature of the *My World* screens is that they take over the whole of the computer screen. Suddenly all the task bars have gone! This is deliberate because it helps prevent the child from playing with other aspects of the computer screen. You can access the menu and escape from the *My World* screen simply by pressing the **Alt** button on your computer's keyboard. This immediately gives you a menu (see Fig. 4.5) that allows you to carry out a number of functions:

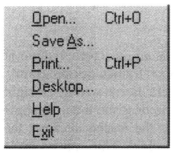

Figure 4.5 The *My World*
menu

Open brings up a list of other *My World* programs on your computer.
Save As allows you to save the screen in an appropriate file or even on the **A** drive.
Print sends the screen to the printer.
Desktop is useful because it restores the menu bars and allows the screen to be used in exactly the same way as any other *Windows* program.
Help gives you the help area.
Exit will close the program. When you click on this a dialog box will appear to ask if you would like to save the current screen.

Using the *My World* programs with children

The expected outcomes of this activity are that the children will explain why they made their decisions and choices; explain how their representations differ from real life; understand that the computer can be used to represent real situations. Children need to learn that a computer can be used to represent real or fantasy situations. To do this we need to present them with opportunities to talk about the differences between the world they see on the computer screen and the real world. The ideal tool for this is a fantasy program or simulation such as the *Find Teddy* screen. In this activity the children are asked to find a teddy (see Fig. 4.6).

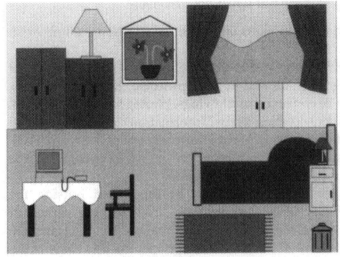

Figure 4.6   The *Find Teddy* screen

You will need a real teddy in the classroom so that you can make real comparisons. In the starting screen the teddy is hidden behind the cupboard doors. The children can click on the different objects in the room and move them. Talk about how the things move and ask if you could move the things in the same way at home. When they have found the teddy they can try to hide it under the different things in the room. Click on the carpet and move it over the teddy. Ask the children about hiding the teddy behind the curtains. Talk about how it would be the same or different with the real teddy.

Children need to know that information exists in different forms. In *Children Using Computers* (Straker and Govier 1996), Anita Straker looks at children's perceptions about information and quotes some information volunteered by children when they were asked what they knew about blood. The following statements were made:

Activity 4.5
The information around us

- 'keeps you alive
- Mum skreems at it
- a red liquid that vampires and Dracular likes
- underneath the skin
- it is different shades of red
- clots
- warm'

Discussing this information invariably leads to questions, which lead to the seeking of more information. In the account above the following questions were asked:

- 'Do insects have blood?
- How much blood have we got inside us?
- Why is blood red?
- Why does blood come out when you fall over?'

This then led on to discussions on where the additional information could be found.

Children need to know that information exists in a variety of forms, including text, still and moving pictures, charts and sounds. Information can be conveyed in drawings, photographs and in signs. What does the zebra crossing tell us? Information can be conveyed in writing in its different forms. What information does the word STOP convey? In this activity the children are going to prepare a tape recording of sounds that carry information.

ICT is not just about computers. In the world outside the classroom the study of ICT incorporates the use of a variety of devices that communicate and carry information. In the classroom, tape recorders, television, video and telephones are just some of the ICT devices that can work independently of a computer and which children should be encouraged to explore.

Working with children investigating sound

The outcomes for this work are to recognise that sounds convey information and to use a cassette recorder to collect and store information as sound. Make sure that you know how the tape recorder works. Record a few sounds before starting the session with the children. These sounds will be sounds that convey a message such as the school bell, a baby crying, a telephone ringing, the siren of a police car. Also plan how you are going to introduce the topic and what questions you will ask.

A good way to start an activity like this one is to give each child a postcard-size piece of card and a pencil and get them to sit quietly in a corner of the classroom and listen. Ask them to draw all the sounds that they can hear. After two to three minutes you can talk about all the sounds around you. What did they tell you? Now play the tape recording and ask the children to close their eyes. Get them to describe the message the sounds are giving them. Can they think of any other sounds that give messages? Make sure that the children see you using the tape recorder and talk about what you are doing and what the result of your actions are. Give them opportunities for pressing the buttons and exploring the device. Do they know where the sound is coming from? Do they know how to make it louder?

Further reading   Straker, Anita and Heather Govier (1996) *Children Using Computers* (2nd edn). Oxford: Nash Pollock Publishing.

Chapter 5

Using ICT to Support Literacy

The early learning goals for language and literacy are linked to the objectives set out in *The National Literacy Strategy: Framework for Teaching* (DfEE 1998). From the perspective of ICT the most important of these are that children should be:

- listening with enjoyment and responding to stories, songs and other music, rhymes and poems and making up their own stories, songs, rhymes and poems;
- using language to imagine and recreate roles and experiences;
- extending their vocabulary, exploring the meanings and sounds of new words;
- retelling narratives in their correct sequence and drawing on the language patterns of stories;
- attempting writing for various purposes, using features of different forms such as lists, stories and instructions.

After the foundation stage the teacher is guided in the classroom literacy work by the National Literacy Strategy. At the core of the framework is a set of teaching objectives divided into year groups, then subdivided into terms. In addition to the planning model, the National Literacy Strategy document gives schools guidance on structuring the delivery of the literacy strategy in a 'Literacy Hour'. The Literacy Hour is divided into the following components:

1. 15 minutes whole class shared text work
2. 15 minutes whole class word level work
3. 20 minutes group and independent work
4. 10 minutes session to feedback

Unless the class is in the unenviable position of possessing technology such as an interactive whiteboard and a projector that can be linked to a computer (point and show device), the main opportunity for using ICT to support the Literacy Hour is through group and independent work.

Activity 5.1 Using the My World software to support early learning literacy goals

Using the *My World* programs is discussed in detail in Chapter 4, Activity 4.4. An example of a screen is shown in Figure 5.1. The screen is designed as a focus for language development and to reinforce the identification of the initial letters of words. It uses the vowel, consonant, and vowel structure of many common objects. It allows words to be 'built' on-screen to match the pictures.

Figure 5.1   A *My World* screen

As with all *My World* activities, the screens are intended as a focus for language development and will not correct the child if s/he makes an error. Any screen may be saved and/or printed through the menu, so that a record of the child's work may be kept.

Using the *My World* screen with children

The outcomes for this activity are linked to the child's recognition of letter shapes and common three-letter words. The children will also be able to click and drag. Make sure that you use the program before using it with the children. Plan your session with the teacher. It is important that you are aware of the stages of development of the children with respect to mouse skills. They must understand the idea of cause and effect to be able to gain anything from this program. Think about the instructions that you are going to give to the children and the language that you will use. Write this down in your planning.

Helping the children to click and drag

Although the *My World* program that you will be using may have the simple click and drag technique described in Activity 4.4, some of the older *My World* programs require the full skill to be used. To help children click and drag get them to hold the mouse and put your hand over theirs. Ask them to move the mouse so that the arrow (cursor) is on top of an object on the screen. Without moving the mouse ask them to click the left-hand button of the mouse with their forefinger and hold it down. At this point you can press on the child's finger to help him/her hold the button down. The mouse can now be moved across the mouse mat. As the mouse moves you will be able to see that the object under the mouse cursor also moves. When the object is where you or the child want it to be, lift the finger off the mouse button. The object will now stay where you left it.

Encourage children to talk about their work. Ask questions such as:

- What is the initial letter of 'ink'?
- What do you think that the word 'ink' has in common (shares) with the words 'ant' and 'arrow'?
- Can you think of any other words starting with the same sound?

Ask open questions which give the children the opportunity to talk about the answer rather than just give a 'yes' or 'no' answer. Offer constructive feedback by using appropriate language to describe what the children are doing. Make time during the activity to talk to individual children. Ask them about what they are doing.

Evaluate your work by thinking back on what you did and quickly write down a sentence about:

- What the children managed to do.
- What you did to facilitate this.
- What you would change if you did it again.

Some children may have difficulty using a keyboard and in most cases when working with early years children most of the keyboard is irrelevant. You may find that the class teacher has set up a concept or overlay keyboard linked to the computer which is used instead of a keyboard (see Fig. 5.2). A concept/overlay keyboard is a pressure-sensitive board consisting of a set of contact switches covered by a flexible membrane. There are usually up to a maximum of 256 switches all linked to their own little square of surface. The concept/overlay keyboard is usually linked to the computer by plugging it into the serial port (the latest boards are linked using an infra-red connection and are therefore wireless). The overlay keyboard does not use mains electricity so you will not need to plug it in anywhere.

How is it used? The computer has a program that allows it to 'talk' to the concept/overlay keyboard. When this is used you can link areas of the overlay keyboard to actions on the computer. For early years children the squares are often linked together to form much larger squares or rectangles like that illustrated in Figure 5.2. Here

Activity 5.2
Using a concept or overlay keyboard to support early learning literacy goals

the overlay contains pictures and symbols. In the overlay in Figure 5.3 the child can press on the words and these can then be made to appear in the word-processing program on the computer. An overlay keyboard with pictures of different fruits and vegetables is used on weighing scales in some supermarkets.

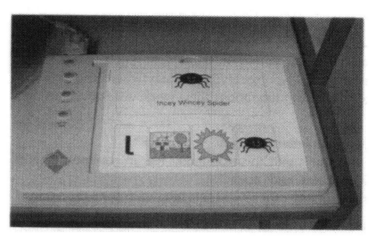

Figure 5.2   An overlay keyboard

Jasbinder	went	ran	garden
tree	up	space	hill
the	I	Spot	road
space	↵	and	print

Figure 5.3   An overlay word bank

Using the concept or overlay keyboard with children

You will need to organise a flat surface area near the computer where you can lay the keyboard. With the most recent keyboards you can use the ordinary keyboard at the same time so your teacher might give you a mixed ability group which will allow the children to interact by using both devices. Make sure that the overlay keyboard is connected to the computer. To prevent damage to the computer or to the concept/overlay keyboard, always shut down and switch off the power to the computer before connecting or disconnecting the cable.

Figure 5.3 illustrates an overlay that your teacher might have created. You will need to make sure that a suitable word-processing program is running. The overlay keyboard then needs to be pressed in the appropriate places and the words appear on the computer monitor.

Encouraging children to talk about their work

Talk to the children about the words. Overlays are versatile in that they can be changed or adapted, so you could add pictures to the overlay words. Describe what the symbols in the bottom row mean. Using computers involves the use of a lot of symbols and every opportunity should be taken to explain these to the children. When the children have discussed the words you can begin to make up the story. At this point it would be possible to develop the story using two groups – one group using the overlay keyboard with the other using the conventional QWERTY keyboard. Each group could take turns to add to the story.

The concept/overlay keyboard is an excellent tool for working with children for whom English is their second language. Do not underestimate the importance of children's home language. Although they may not yet be able to read the words, the concept/overlay keyboard can still be programmed with their home language. Ask a parent for help.

Activity 5.3
Using the Internet to support early learning literacy goals

This activity could be linked to Activity 5.5 where the children are invited to communicate with Sebastian Swan (see later). The Internet is progressively becoming a major teaching and learning resource and it is planned that by 2002 every classroom in the UK will be linked to the Internet. The Internet can be used as a library, a publishing medium or as a communication device. It is important that you become a familiar and confident user of at least the library and communication aspects of the Internet.

For the library of information the Internet is accessed through World Wide Web pages. These multimedia sources of information are held on computers all over the world. The information on the WWW can be accessed by the computer in your classroom using a software program called a browser. The two popular browsers are *Microsoft Internet Explorer* and *Netscape Communicator* and the WWW pages are displayed in the browser interface. Chapter 3 gives you more information on these browsers. The image shown in Figure 5.4 is the early years interface of the Birmingham Grid for Learning displayed in the *Microsoft Internet Explorer* browser window.

The browser window has some important features:

- The address of the WWW page – this can be typed in.
- The **Back** button which will take you back to the page you have just come from.
- If you have gone back then the **Forward** button will take you forward again.
- The **Search** button will take you to a search engine which might help you find the WWW site that you are searching for.
- The **Print** button will print any page that you happen to be on.

Figure 5.4 An example of early years WWW material

The Internet can also be used for communication using email. If you click on **Mail** on the browser menu bar the communication program on the computer should start. Figure 5.5 shows the email software *Microsoft Outlook Express*. Click on the icon **Compose Message** and another window will appear in front of the original one. This is where you can type your message (see Fig. 5.6). In the **To** box type the address of the person you are sending the email to, Mike.Farmer@uce.ac.uk for example. Notice that it has an '@' after the name – this is a characteristic of all email addresses. The 'uce.ac.uk' indicates that the Internet Service Provider (ISP) is the University of Central England (UCE) and that it is an academic institution (ac) based in the UK. In the **Subject** box type what the email is about. It could be that you are getting your group to send a message to some other part of the school so type 'Mrs Farmer's group'. Then type the message.

At the point of writing you could use an overlay keyboard to input the words. You do not need to be connected to the Internet when the email is being typed – the only point at which you have to be connected is when you decide to send the email.

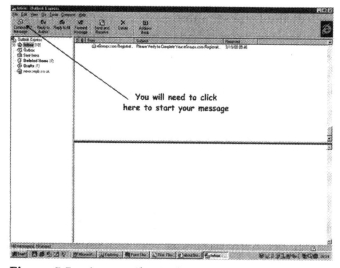

Figure 5.5 An email window

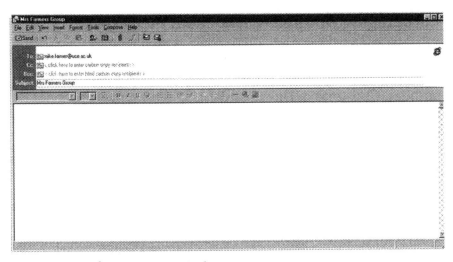

Figure 5.6 The message window

Using email with children

The outcomes of this activity is that the children will be able to identify text/words and know that they can communicate information; use a word bank to create simple sentences; understand that computers can be used to communicate with other people. Check that the computer you will be using with the children is linked to the Internet and that you are familiar with the computer's browser software and email program. Find out the address of the class that you want to send the email to. For the children it will be just as exciting sending an email to someone in the next classroom as it would be to someone a lot farther away. Make sure that you time the exercise to coincide with the other class being on-line – children will want a fairly instant response in this first exercise at communicating outside of the classroom. The class teacher will have prepared an overlay keyboard with text suitable for the communication exercise.

Figure 5.7 illustrates an overlay that your teacher might have created. You will need to make sure that a suitable email program is running. When the concept/overlay keyboard is pressed in the appropriate places the words will appear in the email message area.

we	Mrs Farmer's	an	reply
are	group	email	who
in	and	you	Space
to	sending	please	print

Figure 5.7 An overlay for an email message

Encouraging children to talk about their work

The children should be asked about the ways in which they normally communicate with each other. Do any of them send or receive birthday, Christmas or Diwali cards? Do they use the telephone? Do they shout at children who are a long way away? How can we talk to the children in the other classroom?

Activity 5.4
Using a CD-ROM
to support the
literacy strategy

There is a vast collection of CD-ROMs which can be used to support the National Literacy Strategy and included in this is a range of CD-ROM books. The CD-ROMs can be used as big books if a big enough computer monitor or a computer-linked projector is available. In all likelihood, the CD-ROMs that you will be asked to use have already been used in the classroom. When you start the computer you will probably see a small window which has within it a set of icons; each icon corresponds to a particular CD-ROM. Place the CD–ROM in the CD tray, close it and then click on the CD-ROM corresponding icon. This will start the program.

The program does not start. There could be a number of reasons for this. First check that you have put the CD-ROM in the correct way up. Usually the CD-ROM has a label on it which should be at the top. It might be that the CD-ROM is not sitting correctly in the drive. Don't be frightened to give the disk a firm push onto the drive shaft – you should hear it click into position. Yet another problem occurs if you are too efficient! Once the CD-drive has been closed the drive has to engage with the rest of the computer. If you click on the CD-ROM icon too quickly you may get an error message saying it cannot find drive **D** or **E**, in which case click the **Retry** button. Finally if the CD-ROM is damaged it will not play. You can check that there is nothing wrong with the CD drive by trying it out with another CD-ROM.

Using the CD-ROM with children

Make sure that the CD-ROM you are using is included in the window on the monitor and check that the sound is switched on (Chapter 2). Put the CD-ROM in the CD tray and close it. Try to make sure that you have an opportunity of using the CD-ROM before using it with children to check on all the different things that could happen. Make a few notes about them, particularly the vocabulary that the children will be introduced to.

A popular range of CD-ROMs used for Literacy Hour support are the Living Books series published by Broderbund. The book used in this example, *Sheila Rave the Brave*, links to the topic 'Ourselves'. Sheila Rave is a mouse who was initially afraid of nothing until she decided to set up home in unfamiliar surroundings. The activity is linked to the following outcomes which in themselves give clues to the way in which you might be expected to interact with the children. The activity will:

- develop an awareness of a story with a sequence of events;
- develop listening skills;
- provide stimuli for conversation between adults and other children;
- develop turn taking.

Introduce the story to the children and then explain how they will interact with the pictures on the screen. All *Living Library* screens have a similar level of interaction. When entering a screen there is an animation and then the children are invited to explore the screen to find more hidden animations before going to the next page. Try to ensure that you offer constructive feedback. After all the activities on the first screen have been completed talk to the children about what happened and what might happen on the next screen. This story could provide a stimulus to encourage children to talk about feeling happy/sad, friendships and having friends. When the children are talking about what will happen and what might happen, listen and comment on their suggestions. Do not dismiss their comments even though they may be imaginative. You will have the opportunity of discussing their suggestions when the next scene appears. At this point the children can look back and comment on their own predictions.

If you are working with children for whom English is their second language discuss with the teacher any new words that might arise in going through the program. The teacher will advise you of the important new words on which to focus. When a new thing happens on the screen explain to the children what you see happening. Encourage the child to use the new word in the discussion about what is going to happen on the next page. Make sure that you offer praise for each new word that the child tries to use.

Activity 5.5
Using big books on the WWW to support the literacy strategy

The WWW is fast becoming a place where teachers can find information to support the literacy strategy. There are already several big books on-line which the teacher might read with the children and which could then be used for either group or independent learning activities. In most cases the computer you will be using will be connected to the Internet and therefore you may be accessing the WWW directly. Like all computer-based activities this can cause difficulties if things go wrong. For example the Internet connection may be so busy that everything seems to be happening at a snail's pace. A small blue bar at the bottom of the browser will tell you how fast the page you want to look at is loading (coming from the distant computer to your computer). If it is moving very slowly you will know that you will have to work extra hard to entertain the children!

Another problem is that the site which hosts the WWW pages could be having problems and you will end up with a blank screen and an error message. To avoid this ask the IT Coordinator to 'download' the pages that you want to use onto the school network. This can be done by using a program like *Teleport Pro* (Tenmax) found at http://www.tenmax.com which will quickly download hundreds of pages. An alternative method is to make sure you access the WWW pages before you show them to your teaching group. Why? Firstly it makes good sense to go through what you might be doing with the children. Secondly it gives you an opportunity of checking the address of the site you want to access. Finally, accessing the site with the computer will load all the pages that you visit into its short-term memory (called a cache). This will allow you to access the site off-line if things do go wrong.

In this activity the *Sebastian Swan* site has its own special method for downloading. Go to the site and follow the comprehensive instructions. Make sure that the site you plan to access is in the **Favorites** (notice American spelling) or **Bookmark** file of your browser. This file is where you keep the addresses of all your important WWW sites. When you visit a site which you may think is going to be useful, click on **Favorites/Bookmark** on the top bar of your browser. When a dialog box appears click on **Add To Favorites**. Click on the button and the site address is now added to the list. When you want to access the WWW site in the future all you will need to do is go to the **Favorites/Bookmark** icon on the navigation bar and find the name of the site.

Using WWW big books with children

In this activity you will be using a big book available at http://www.naturegrid.org.uk/infant/bigbook.html on the Kent Grid for Learning. Click on *Sebastians Waddle*. This will bring up a big book consisting of a series of text and photographs about the movement of Sebastian (see Fig. 5.8).

Make sure that you have visited the WWW site and all the pages that you might be using. The site has some interesting hyperlinks (cross-references) that take you and the children to more information on the text used. This makes it doubly important that you examine the site before working with it with children (see Fig. 5.9). To save

Figure 5.8   The *Sebastian Swan* site

time, make sure that the computer has been turned on in advance of the lesson. You may want to use the session to show children how to start the web browser and how to log-on and access *Sebastian Swan* books. If the teacher is going to ask children to follow up this activity for themselves, you may be asked to show them how to use the browser so that they will be able to find the pages they need.

Figure 5.9   A hyperlink in the *Sebastian Swan* story

Before you start, consider carefully where you position yourself so that you can use the mouse and keyboard. Sitting to one side of the computer with the keyboard on your lap will enable you to face the group and be fully involved in the discussion. You may also need to position the screen, or the children, so that everyone can see it clearly. Try it out beforehand and check that there are no reflections from windows or other light sources that may make it difficult for all of the children to see the screen. Closing blinds or curtains, if you have them, may help cut down on reflections. An area of discussion with respect to this task could be 'How is this different from a book?' You could ask questions such as:

- Who wrote it?
- Is there a title page?
- Is there a contents page or index?

Discuss with the children how they can turn the page so that they go forward and backward in the book. Later find an example of a hyperlink (an underlined word in blue) and show how this can move the reader from one page to another.

Reinforcing learning

It is important that children quickly develop the skills of using WWW pages so make sure that all the children in your group have an opportunity of moving the mouse, watching the cursor change from an arrow to a hand, and then clicking on the hyperlink. Talk to the children about what has happened and why. Show them how you can get back to where you came from. Make sure that you use the correct language and explain it when you are helping the children. This activity could be linked to Activity 5.3 since the *Sebastian Swan* books have an email link at the end of each book. This could be a useful stimulus to talk about communication and lead into this activity.

Activity 5.6 Using word-processing software to support the literacy strategy

Probably one of the most important programs that you use with children will be the word processor. In its simplest form a word processor allows text to be entered via a keyboard which then appears on a monitor (simulating a piece of paper). The text can then be printed onto a 'real' piece of paper. You may ask why it is important that children use a computer to produce text when there are a lot cheaper and easier ways of producing it – paper and pencil have in the past produced some excellent writing. There are some good reasons why teachers encourage the use of computers in this text production process.

The most important reason is that a computer allows the text to be edited quickly and effectively. Children can review and refine their work and make changes without the 'rubbing and crossing out' that usually accompanies paper and pencil writing. Whole chunks of text can be moved around. Sentences can be easily moved from the beginning to the end of a paragraph, and when it is found that it makes less sense than it did before it can be moved back. Word processing can be used to actively encourage children to draft and redraft work and therefore interact more meaningfully with the text. Other benefits include the spell check facility and the enhancement of text presentation by the use of different font sizes and font types as well as alignment and colour options. Some word processors also have a sound facility which allow the children to hear the word they are typing. You may find that, for young children, hunting around the keyboard for letters is a slow process, so it is important that they are given the opportunity of working with a small amount of text.

Familiarising yourself with the word processor

To support children when they are using a word processor means that you must be familiar with the way in which it is used. The most important tasks that you will be involved in when using a word processor are:

- loading the program onto the computer;
- changing the size of the font on the screen;
- entering text;
- using the space bar;
- using the shift key punctuation marks;
- word wrap and enter/return key;
- saving work to the hard drive and to a floppy disk.

Switch on the computer. When the program icons appear look for the word-processing icon and double click on it start the program. Most word processors have a pictorial menu (tool) bar near the top of the screen that allows you to carry out most of the operations in the list above (see Fig. 5.10).

Figure 5.10 The word-processor tool bar

Nothing happens when I try to change the text. This is probably because you have not highlighted it. To change the characteristics of most text in word processors you need to highlight the text (see Fig. 5.11). Highlighting an individual word can sometimes be done by double clicking on it. Alternatively, a more difficult option, is to move the text cursor to the front of the word, hold down the left mouse button and using the mouse drag the cursor across the text. You will then see the text highlighted. Let go of the mouse button when you have finished. Once the text is highlighted you will be able to change the font characteristics.

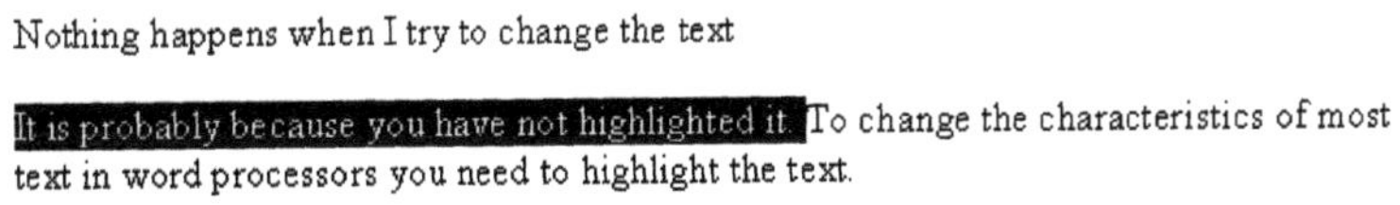

Nothing happens when I try to change the text

It is probably because you have not highlighted it. To change the characteristics of most text in word processors you need to highlight the text.

Figure 5.11 Highlighted text

The space bar at the front of the keyboard is used to create spaces between words while the shift key changes lower case letters to upper case. If the **Shift** key (on some keyboards this key is indicated by an arrow symbol ⇨) is held down while a letter is being typed the letter is upper case. Let go of the **Shift** key and the letters typed return to lower case. If you want to type completely in upper case press the **Caps Lock** key. Pressing this key again removes the restriction. A very important key is the **Enter/Return** key. On some keyboards it is called the **Enter** or **Return** key while on others it is indicated by an arrow symbol ⏎ . This is important in word processing because it moves the text cursor down to another line. This is necessary when a new paragraph is required, but in normal use the computer will automatically move the text cursor down to the next line when it reaches the edge of the 'virtual' page – this process is called 'word wrapping'.

Saving work

When the children have produced some work it needs to be saved. Work should be saved at regular intervals all the way through the creation process, not just on completion of the work. The way in which work is saved depends either on the school or your class teacher's policy. Physically there are two places to save work on a computer – the hard disk and the floppy disk (or both). Sometimes this is complicated further by a policy of saving work on the main network computer (server). Whatever the policy, look for either the picture of the floppy disk in the pictorial menu bar or go to the word **File** in the top menu bar.

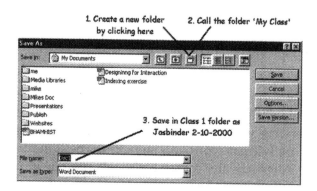

Figure 5.12   Beginning to save your work

In both cases clicking on these options presents you with a dialog box which will give you one of the most worrying but important lessons when using a computer.

What on earth does it mean? The picture above illustrates one of the author's complex filing systems and the computer is effectively asking 'Where do you want to save this work in this mess?' to which the correct answer is 'There isn't anywhere suitable'. Your class teacher, or you, will therefore create a new folder by clicking on the **New Folder** button (see Figure 5.12). Type 'Class 1' into the **Name** box and click **OK**. This will give you a *Class 1* folder in the **Save As** box. Double clicking on this will give you a neat and tidy area in which you can save Jasbinder's work. Make sure that you give the work a specifically unique name so that it can be distinguished from the other children's work and also from other work that Jasbinder could be doing. Sometimes the date is used, for example 'jasbinder 2-10-2000'. For more information on saving work see Chapter 10.

Saving work to a floppy disk

It is sometimes useful to save the children's work on a floppy disk. If the work is also saved on the computer network there is the added security that the work is saved in two places. Ask your teacher or the IT Coordinator for a floppy disk and make sure that you also get a label – unlabelled disks can cause all sorts of problems which are best avoided. Put the disk into the disk drive (do not worry about putting it in the wrong way around, it will not let you) and then instead of going to the **Save** icon, go to the **File** label at the top of the screen and click on the word **File**. A dropdown menu appears. Move the mouse cursor down to **Save As** and click on the word. The **Save As** dialog box appears. Go to the top of the dialog box and click on the small downward arrow at the end of the **Save In** box. Scan through the list and click on the **A**. Name the piece of work and click on the **Save** button to save the work

I get a message telling me something is wrong. The most common message is something like 'Cannot read from **A**' or 'The drive is not in use'. This means that you have probably not put the disk into the drive. Make sure the disk is in the drive and try again. Another common message is that the disk is full. If this happens get an empty disk from your teacher. Floppy disks can only store a limited amount of information and if you are saving pictures or drawings these take up a lot of space.

Working with the children: creating and editing a story

The outcomes of this session are that the children will be able to recognise some of the features of word-processed text, enter and correct text, and understand that spaces need to be placed between words. In this exercise you are helping the children to create a story about pets. All the stories will then be collected and brought together as a book about pets.

Your first task will be to remind the children about some of the functions of a word processor. Type in a few words that have no spaces between them such as 'Ihavetwoblackandwhitecats'. Remind the children how to put spaces into the text and show them how to place the cursor and use the space bar (remind children that they use their fingers to create spaces between words in their hand-written work). Misspell a couple of the words that you type in and get the children to check the text using the spell checker. Talk to the children about how the words can be corrected. Get them to show you how to place the cursor and use the **BkSp** (Back Space) key (may be indicated by an arrow symbol ⇦). If the teacher has not already done it for you, create a word bank on 'word cards' to support the children in their story-making.

Further reading

Birmingham City Council (2000) *Developing Good Practice in the Use of ICT in the Early Years' Classroom.* Birmingham: Birmingham City Council.

DfEE (1998) *The National Literacy Strategy: Framework for Teaching.* London: DfEE.

Chapter 6

Using ICT to Support Numeracy and Mathematics

The daily mathematics lesson follows a time pattern similar to the Literacy Hour:

1. 10 minutes mental/oral session
2. 30 minutes focused mathematics session
3. 10 minutes plenary

ICT would mainly be used in the focused mathematics session, but if your teacher is having difficulty finding mental maths activities there is a WWW site at http://www.ginn.co.uk/mathematics/ which contains a wealth of ideas. If you have become competent in using the WWW you could offer to look at the above site on a weekly or even daily basis for mental maths ideas. ICT can present opportunities for observing patterns, developing visual imagery and, in particular, an understanding of how to express instructions in a clear and precise way.

Activity 6.1
Supporting
counting skills
using ICT

ICT can offer considerable support in learning involving repetition and practice. Imagine a group of children having problems in reciting the numbers from 13 to 19 and transitions, such as that from 29 to 30. A number line is essential in the development of these skills but even then some children have touch counting skills which can lead to an incorrect total at the end of a count. This activity aims to improve children's counting skills through the use of a painting program such as *Paint it* (JETSoft) or *Kid Pix* (Broderbund). Both of these and other software painting programs have a facility that lets children stamp pictures onto a screen (see Fig. 6.1). Using *Kid Pix* it is not only possible to stamp different shapes on the screen, it is also possible to stamp numbers which can then be spoken. An alternative program, *Clicker* (Crick Software), also provides the same facility if *Kid Pix* is not available.

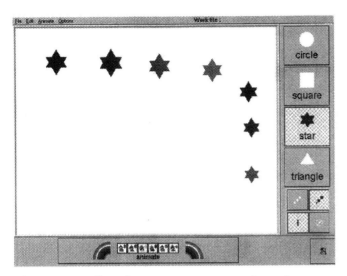

Figure 6.1 Creating your own counting picture

Using the counting activity with children

Check that you know what the activity involves. As part of this process you will have talked to the teacher and agreed on the outcomes for the activity. In this instance the outcomes are that the children will practise using their counting vocabulary and improve the reliability of their counting; develop their mouse skills and recognise that computers can assist them in their learning.

On the screen will be a couple of large shapes such as a triangle and square. In the first instance you present the children with the 'real' small shapes that match the larger on-screen shapes (triangle or square). You then ask the children to add to each on-screen shape the shape you have produced, using the appropriate object stamp. Encourage the children to count the number of objects that are included within each shape as they are added. When enough objects have been added ask the children to repeat the counting – this encourages systematic counting. Make sure that the children count out loud to enable them to use the software more independently. When the counting picture is complete, print it out so that the children can share it and also take it home.

Before proceeding with this activity you should read Chapter 4, Activity 4.4, which gives full details on using the *My World* programs. A screen that supports numeracy is shown in Figure 6.2 and can be used for shape work and tessellation. The screen is used to support the understanding of the square and the triangle. Children can click on the different squares on the right-hand side of the screen, move the shape across to the left-hand side and by clicking once more can drop the shape into a particular position. This screen also has an advanced option that allows the shape to be rotated.

Activity 6.2
Using the **My World** *software to support early numeracy goals*

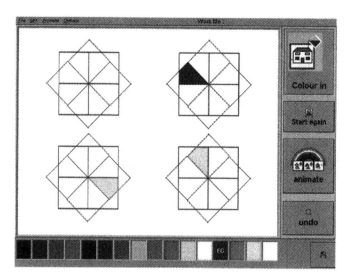

Figure 6.2   Tessellations

Using the *My World* screen with children

Make sure that you have tried out the computer program before using it with the children. Remember that the **Alt** button on the keyboard gives you access to the control panel. If you want to print the final pattern check that the printer is working. Create a simple pattern on the screen and print it. Plan the steps that you are going to take and talk these over with the teacher. Talk to the children about the shapes and show them how they can be picked up and moved and also how they can get rid of unwanted objects. Talk about the pattern that you want to make. One shape will rest against another shape. Show them a pattern that you had made earlier and get the children (one at a time) to add to the pattern. As they move the shapes make sure they tell you what shape it is.

Encouraging children to talk about their work

You should ask questions such as:

- What are the names of the shapes?
- Can you make patterns with the shapes?
- How could you use triangles to make squares?
- What do you think will happen if the triangle is turned round?

Ask open questions which give the children the opportunity to talk about the answer rather than a simple 'yes' or 'no'.

All Key Stage 1 children are expected to experience 'control'. What does this mean? Is it about discipline? Unfortunately it is not that simple – it is about control using computers. When people who regularly use computers talk about control they mean electronic control. For example, when you use a modern washing machine and set the controller for a woollen wash, the controller controls the temperature that the water reaches and the length of time that the garment stays in the washing and rinsing cycle. The device that establishes and checks on the behaviour of the washing machine is a little computer that is practising control.

Children experience control with many modern toys. The *Furby* is a toy that has a substantial control element in its make-up. If you clap your hands sound sensors make it wake up. If you stroke its back, pressure sensors make it tell you that it 'loves you'. If you put your hand in its mouth as a response to a 'feed me' command it responds by thanking you and asking for more. This is control! In the early years classroom we are looking at the early stages of experiencing control and the most common of these is the floor turtle or roamer (see Fig. 6.3). The floor turtle or roamer is a toy which can be made to travel forward, backward, to the left, to the right and to pause by keying in simple instructions using a small keyboard on the control panel (see Fig. 6.4).

Activity 6.3
Using roamers to support the numeracy strategy

Figure 6.3   A roamer on the move

Figure 6.4   The control panel

Using the floor turtle/roamer

The instructions that you feed into the roamer/turtle are a form of programming language called *Logo*. *Logo* is demanding for Key Stage 1 children and for many at the lower end of Key Stage 2. However, programmable robots like the floor turtle or roamer can be used to lay valuable foundations for future *Logo* work and in the long term will give children insights into how computers work. The control panel in the roamer/turtle has a series of keys that are used to deliver the programming that takes the roamer/turtle through its motions. One of the most important is the **CM** key, which is used right at the start of any programming. This key clears the memory in the roamer turtle. The next stage is to give the turtle its instructions using the Keys shown in Figures 6.5–6.8.

To make the turtle/roamer move forward press

Figure 6.5   Making the roamer/turtle move forwards

To make the turtle/roamer move backward press

Figure 6.6   Making the roamer/turtle move backwards

To make the turtle/roamer turn right press

Figure 6.7   Making the roamer/turn right (clockwise)

To make the turtle/roamer turn left press

Figure 6.8   Making the roamer/turtle turn left (anticlockwise). After pressing each key a number is entered using the control panel. This number denotes the number of moves or units you want the roamer/turtle to take in that direction.

When you are ready for the turtle/roamer to carry out your instructions press **GO**. One roamer measurement unit will move the roamer forward by 30cm, 90 roamer turning units will rotate the roamer through 90° or a right angle. The following set of instructions will cause the roamer to complete a square, each side being 10 roamer units long:

1. Forward 10
2. Turn right 90
3. Forward 10
4. Turn right 90
5. Forward 10
6. Turn right 90
7. Forward 10

The **P** (Pause) and **R** (Repeat) key allow for more sophisticated programming.

My roamer keeps doing a triangle before it does what I've told it to do. Whenever a roamer is switched on it will perform its demonstration program when the **GO** key is pressed. To get rid of the demonstration program press **CM** twice. *I cannot cancel my roamer's memory.* The **CM** key button needs to be pressed twice to clear the memory (to avoid cancelling programs by mistake). *My roamer doesn't do a proper square.* The roamer's accuracy can be affected by the surface it is running on. In Figure 6.3 the roamer has a special surface on which it can move but it will never have the precision accuracy of the turtle. *My roamer is going around in circles.* This is usually due to battery problems.

Using a roamer with children

In this activity the children will recognise that control devices follow instructions; enter instructions to control the roamer; predict the results of different instructions. Make sure that the roamer contains a good set of batteries in it – looking for new batteries can be difficult in the middle of a lesson with a group of young children. Make sure that you know how the roamer operates i.e. that you have already tried using it before starting the activity with your group. Discuss the basic instructions needed by the roamer to make it move and show the children how to enter the instructions. They will need to be shown how to clear the memory and how to enter instructions one at a time.

Talk to the whole group about what they are going to do. Show them how to plot a route of:

1. Start
2. Forward 2
3. Turn right 90
4. Forward 2
5. Turn left 90
6. Forward 6
7. Turn right 90
8. Forward 20
9. Turn left 90

10. Pause 10
11. Forward 5
12. Turn left 90

One group is then set to create a pathway for the roamer using six interlocking mats, while the other group work on the activity on a prepared worksheet. At the changeover the worksheet group control the roamer while the planning group complete the worksheet.

Encouraging talk

Talk to the children about left and right, forward and backward and pause. Be aware that the children may not be aware of the language involved in this activity. Question the children about how they think the roamer will move and ask them to talk about the movements. Your teacher may have given the children preparatory activities, such as the physical movement around obstacle courses or paper-based exercises in which they have to talk about how they are getting from one place to another. In these cases talking about the movement will reinforce previous learning.

Activity 6.4
Using the WWW
to support the
numeracy strategy

The WWW provides teachers with an excellent source of information to support the National Numeracy Strategy. During the 30-minute focused mathematics session, the teacher is encouraged to include mathematical games that are guided by the framework objectives (DfEE) 1999). There are progressively more and more WWW sites being developed to support teachers in this area. A good source that offers ideas on how to support the numeracy strategy is at http://www.ginn.co.uk/maths/login.asp the Ginn Mega Mathematics Store site. Type the address in the address box at the top of the browser window and press **Enter** (*Netscape Communicator* or *Microsoft Internet Explorer*). You will be asked to register before being allowed to proceed. This is nothing to worry about – all you need to give is your email address and a few other details. Try to remember your user name (preferably not your own name) and your password.

I get an error message saying that the site cannot be found. The most likely reason is that you have typed the address incorrectly. Make sure there are no spaces in the address – WWW addresses do not like spaces – correct any errors and try again. If you get an error message again it may be that Ginn have changed the site. Type in http://www.ginn.co.uk/ and see if that connects you to the Ginn site. You can then look for the Mega Mathematics area.

Working with children using the WWW – counting to ten

This activity uses http://www.bgfl.org/ the Birmingham Grid for Learning site. This is a large site and you will need to click on **Primary and Early Years** then **Key Stage 1** before you get to the **Learning Activities**. Alternatively you can type in http://www.bgfl.org/bgfl/primary/ks1/learning activites/Numeracy/ks1_numindex.html directly. This will bring you to an activity called *Passengers on a bus*. This activity can be used for developing the child's understanding of number partition up to ten. By placing passengers on the upper and lower decks of a bus the child experiences the different ways that ten objects can be partitioned (see Fig. 6.9). Working independently, the child consolidates his/her number sequencing skills as well as experiencing how to create a variety of different sets of objects (conservation).

Figure 6.9 *Passengers on a bus*

With your support the activity can be extended for assessment purposes by asking the child to place a certain number of passengers on the upper deck and a certain number of passengers on the lower deck. Counting the passengers reinforces the number system while the inclusion of the dynamic sum provides an introduction to addition. You may need to help the children to drag and drop. Remember this is done by clicking the left-hand button of the mouse on an object (in this case a face) and holding the button down . You then move the mouse and the object will move with it. When you get to where you want to go, let go of the button.

Talk to the children about what they are doing. Make sure that you bring their attention to the numbers that appear in the bar across the centre of the bus and in the traffic lights and ask the children what they mean. When the activity is finished you can print the picture by clicking on the **Print** button. Remember that to return to where you were on a WWW page, go to the top of the page and click on the **Back** button. This is an alternative navigation to using the other buttons on the screen.

Activity 6.5
Using a spread-
sheet to support
numeracy work

A spreadsheet is a computer program that is designed to display and process text information and numbers. It is made up from a grid into which numbers are entered. You can then apply lots of different types of calculations to the numbers and display the numbers in the form of graphs. It is the graphical properties that we will be using here as spreadsheets have the ability to produce some remarkable pie charts.

What is a pie chart?

A pie chart is a visual display of data. To draw a pie chart by hand is a very complex process involving a knowledge of ratios, division into 360 and the accurate measurement of angles, but to look at a pie chart and understand its meaning is a relatively easy task. In this exercise the teacher has used a spreadsheet program called *Starting Grid* (Research Machines) to set up a question table (see Fig. 6.10). This program comes in a variety of modes: green, yellow and red. Each of these modes gives the user access to more facilities. For the children you will be working with, the yellow mode is the most appropriate. In this activity we are going to set up a table linked to the children's favourite coloured pencils. Your role is to complete the table using information that the children have given you and then to help them produce a pie chart.

	A	B	C	D	E
1	Red	Blue	Green	Yellow	
2	4	8	3	10	
3					
4					

Figure 6.10 The *Starting Grid* table

Before you do this you may be interested in how the teacher set up the question table. *Starting Grid* is called a spreadsheet program because it can be used to create tables of information on which calculations can be performed. In this instance no calculations are being made so the spreadsheet is just being used as a table. Once the children have collected the information they can take turns in filling in the totals in the table. You can quite easily create another column by moving the mouse to the square **E1** and typing in a new colour followed by the number of pencils in square **E2**. Next look for the **Graph** icon on the tool bar – it could be something like that shown in Figure 6.11. Clicking on the icon presents you with a series of options. Choose **Pie Charts** and a pie chart such as the one illustrated in Figure 6.12 will automatically be drawn. It is important to then discuss the pie chart with the children. What does it mean? Why is the circle split up in the way it is? What does the 'key' (sometimes referred to in software programs as the legend) at the side mean? How is it linked to the pie chart? How does the table relate to the pie chart? Does it show which is the most popular coloured pencil?

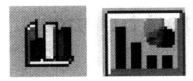

Figure 6.11   Common **Graph** icons

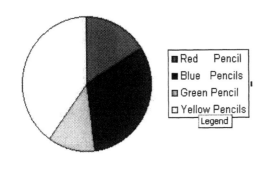

Figure 6.12   A pie chart

DfEE (1999) *National Numeracy Strategy*. London: DfEE Publications.   ***Further reading***

Chapter 7

Using ICT to Support Science

In science you are likely to be using ICT either as a source of information or as a tool to assist in a scientific investigation. There is a large collection of CD-ROMs available that can be used in a variety of ways to help in the teaching of scientific ideas. The class teacher may use them as a class teaching tool if a large monitor is available or alternatively as a research tool for a small group. In the latter case it is likely that you will be involved.

Another ICT skill that you will undoubtedly use in the near future is the digital camera. The digital camera is progressively being used to support early years teaching, and the teaching of children with special needs. It is also proving very useful in science work. The Science National Curriculum states that we should ensure that the science experience of children is linked to scientific enquiry which is taught through contexts taken from the physical and biological world around us (DfEE/QCA 1999). These include life processes and living things, materials and their properties and physical processes such as light, sound and electricity. Through this enquiry children should be involved in:

- Collecting evidence and making observations and measurements to answer questions.
- Planning through asking questions and trying to find answers.
- Obtaining and presenting evidence through using all their senses and through effective communication.
- Considering evidence and evaluating it.

From this list it is apparent that science is a practical subject and as such ICT is a tool which should assist in the investigations but not replace it.

In any science work, the question is probably the hardest yet the most important item to formulate. In this example of a science activity, the importance of the question is emphasised and the use of the word processor allows for refinement and editing of the question. The teacher has produced a plastic container consisting of two large plastic drinks bottles cut in half and sellotaped together (see Fig. 7.1). This provides a useful observation chamber for the small animals that have been collected from a local compost heap (it is important that after the lesson the small animals are returned as quickly as possible to the site where they were found). There are worms, millipedes, woodlice, snails and the odd spider moving around in the container trying to find somewhere to hide. The teacher asks the children to carefully look at the animals and then to imagine that they could speak. 'If the animals that you are looking at could speak, what questions would you like to ask?' The children are then asked to communicate the questions to the rest of the class.

*Activity 7.1
Finding the
question, using a
word-processing
program and word
bank*

Figure 7.1   A small animal observation chamber

The different table groups then take turns in using the word processor to prepare their questions, checking on the form of words. To help in this process, an on-screen word bank can be prepared to support the question formulation.

Using on-screen word banks

An on-screen word bank is a little like a concept keyboard which is described in Chapter 5, Activity 5.2. Instead of using an overlay, the overlay is on the screen itself usually just underneath the word-processing area. An example of an on-screen word bank is the *Clicker* (Crick Software) series of software packages. *Clicker* is essentially a grid that can be made to sit under the word-processing package containing the words that you think will help the children formulate questions (see Fig. 7.2). The words can be added to the grid by holding down the **Shift** key and clicking on the cell in the grid you want to change. This allows you to type in the word or change the existing word. When the children use the grid all they have to do is click on the word and it appears in the word-processing area. They can then quickly build up sentences. The word-processing area can always be used as a word processor in the normal way. Moving the mouse into this area and clicking allows you to resize fonts, colour them and add new words that are not included in the grid. *Clicker* also has a sound facility – if you click on any cell with the right-hand mouse button the word is spoken.

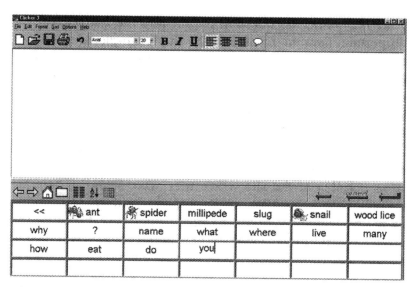

Figure 7.2 An on-screen word bank

Working with children using the word bank

The outcomes for this session will be that the children will be able to formulate and present questions; use an on-screen word bank; use the font size and style facilities. Children are naturally curious so they will come to the computer with a whole collection of questions. Listen to those questions and ask the children to type them into the computer. The next stage is to decide if the questions can be investigated. Ask the children how they might be able to find out the answer. If the question is such that an answer is not possible, talk about how the question might be reworded so that an answer could be found. 'Why have you got two eyes?' could be turned into 'Have all of you got two eyes?'

Show the children how they can change the questions by using the editing facilities of the word processor and then show them how to change the font and the font size so that the questions can be put in a display area. Ask the teacher about the fonts that the school prefers the children to use. The children will now have to present their questions in such a way that they can be displayed. Talk about the size of text and remind them how this can be changed after the text has been highlighted. Show the children three fonts – Times Roman, Arial and Comic Sans – and ask them to choose between them. Why do they like one and not the other? What is the difference between the different fonts?

What is different? There are two basic types of font: Serif and Sans Serif. A serif is the 'cross line' at the end of the letter shape. Look at a letter shape in this book and you will see that each letter has a small crossing line at the end of each stroke. It was not until the beginning of the twentieth century that the Sans Serif font (French for 'without serif') was developed. For young children and the visually impaired, Sans Serif text is recognised as being much easier to use.

Digital cameras are proving to be very useful teaching aids and it is quite likely that at one stage in your work you will be asked to use one (see Fig. 7.3). Digital cameras come in various shapes and sizes but they all have one thing in common – the picture taken is stored in a memory chip in the camera rather than on an ordinary film. The different colours that make up a picture are converted to digital signals by sensors placed behind the lens. This allows the pictures to be displayed directly onto a computer monitor or imported into a graphics or art package for editing. Some cameras store the pictures onto a floppy disk which allows for quick access. Just remove the disk and transfer it to the floppy disk drive of the computer. If the computer has a suitable graphics program such as *Paint Shop Pro* (JASC Software) the pictures can be accessed instantaneously and printed if required. The printed picture is not as good quality as a 'normal' photograph but it is immediately accessible for use.

Activity 7.2
Using a digital camera

Figure 7.3   A digital camera

All the cameras seem to have different ways of accessing the pictures. Usually a lead is required which connects the memory of the camera to the computer base unit. The computer then downloads its pictures. Again a graphics package such as *Paint Shop Pro* would be very useful, but digital camera companies also sell their own graphics handling software packages which can be used to access the photographs. Digital cameras are very similar to ordinary cameras with respect to the way they operate, i.e. they are point and press devices. Most of them have automatic focusing and light control. However, one main difference is that the digital camera can be programmed to take a range of photographs dependent on the quality that is required. The better the picture the more memory it occupies in the camera's memory chip, so high definition photographs mean fewer photographs.

In the classroom the usefulness of the digital camera is linked to the time it takes to replay recorded events. This has been found to be particularly useful in the teaching of very young children or children with special needs where sometimes memory is very short term and children have difficulty recalling the start of a sequence of actions.

The digital camera can show the children the first steps they took in drawing a picture and they can then compare it directly to the finished product. The ability to quickly record and show sequenced events makes the digital camera an invaluable tool in science work in which investigations usually involve change in some way. For example, in an investigation of the melting of ice cubes the children can have a record of the various stages of their ice cube melting.

Using the digital camera with children

In this experiment the camera is going to be used to take photographs of a plant growing. A good plant to grow is buckwheat (usually readily available at health food shops). The advantage of buckwheat is that you can get considerable growth over a two-week period. The children set up their growing experiments in yoghurt pots or other suitable containers, and after talking about how they are going to look after the seeds they are asked how fast they think the plants will grow. At this point the digital camera can be introduced as a way to record the growing:

- When should we take the photographs?
- Should we take them on regular occasions?
- Where shall we place the camera to take the photograph?
- Why do we have to keep the camera still when we are taking a photograph?
- How shall we display the photographs?

All of these questions and more can be tackled before setting out on the investigation.

Most of the cameras are quite robust devices so there is no harm in letting the children, under supervision, take the photographs. Once the camera position has been decided the recording can begin. Most digital cameras have a playback device built into the camera so when the recording period is over the children will be able to see the sequence of events on a small computer screen. This may be an adequate record although for a whole class presentation it is usually better to print the photographs. By whatever means your camera uses, transfer the pictures to the computer and if necessary print them off directly.

The pictures are too big. If you have taken the pictures using a high resolution option the photographs will be very large. The best way to get them to print on the paper is to click on **File** at the top of the screen and move the mouse down to **Print Preview**. In **Print Preview** you will probably find an option that says **Set Up**. This may well include another option called **Fit to Page** – most picture-handling software has this option hidden somewhere in its structure. If everything fails look in the **Help** section of the software or reduce the size of the photograph in a software program like *Paint Shop Pro* (JASC Software).

This exercise focuses on the question 'Where do I live?' Children are expected to produce a folder that will include pictures and lots of information on the environment in which the animal they have adopted lives. For children to answer some of their own questions, research rather than experimentation may be the way forward. CD-ROMs and the WWW can be important sources of information. Although we now have a variety of on-line encyclopedias, including the *Encyclopedia Britannica,* the most popular source of information at Key Stage 1 is probably an encyclopedia like the *Dorling Kindersley Eyewitness Children's Encyclopedia.* Although not a tool for very young children it is excellent for those in Key Stage 1.

Like any CD-ROM you first have to make sure that the Start Up program is installed on the computer that you will be using. CD-ROMs hold so much information that installing it all into the computer memory would soon fill up all the available space. To overcome this a Start Up program is installed on the computer which then retrieves the information from the CD-ROM. This means that if you want to use the encyclopedia you must have access to the encyclopedia CD-ROM. On some of the more modern computer networks in schools, the CD-ROMs are held centrally on a special CD-ROM server so you will be able to access them directly. Your teacher will be able to give you advice on this.

Before using the encyclopedia with the children it is important that you first try using it yourself. The interfaces of any computer-based encyclopedia tend to be fairly complex so it is important that you are familiar with the different parts before you start. Information in interactive encyclopaedias is usually accessible in one of two ways. Firstly, there is a search engine where you can type in either your question or just a key word and ask it to search for anything relating to the question or key word. Secondly there is the directory (menu) structure where you start your search by recognising the broad area in which you think the answer to your question can be found and then slowly refine your search as you move from one menu to another. For example, the *Eyewitness Children's Encyclopedia* has the following main directories:

- Culture
- Nature
- History
- Science
- Geography
- Atlas

Clicking on **Nature** gives a number of other menus such as Plants, Animals, Environment, Weather etc. Clicking on one of these then gives more subdirectories until you eventually reach an area where you will find the answer to the question that you have asked.

Key word searches depend upon the key words or questions asked and this can lead to some important teaching and learning points. All information stored on CD-ROMs and on the WWW search engines

Activity 7.3
Using a CD-ROM
encyclopedia

are databases which have very sophisticated and well-designed graphical interfaces that allow you to search for the information.

Hyperlinks

Another way in which the interactive encyclopaedia can be accessed is via hyperlinks. This is a way of presenting text that allows you to 'jump' around the text by clicking on selected words. Hyperlinks revolutionised the way in which text could be used on computers and gave new freedom to navigate through large quantities of text. If you are uncertain of what a word means in this book you will need to turn the pages and go to the Glossary; if this was being read on a computer you would just need to click on the word and the description of the word would appear. Usually hyperlinked words are highlighted in some way and on WWW pages you will often find them underlined (see Fig. 7.4).

A hyperlink

Figure 7.4 A hyperlink

About databases

Databases are stores of structured information. The best way to store information is in a table, so databases tend to be very large tables with fields along the top and records down the side. Fields are categories of information while records are the collection of fields relating to a particular item. Look at Figure 7.5 below on small animals.

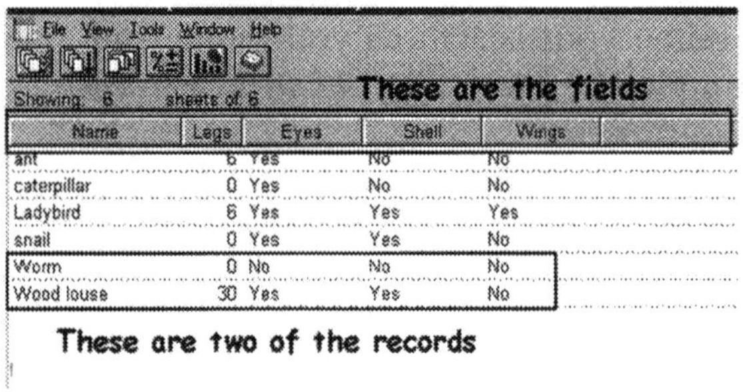

File View Tools Window Help					
Showing: 6 sheets of 6			**These are the fields**		
Name	Legs	Eyes	Shell	Wings	
ant	6	Yes	No	No	
caterpillar	0	Yes	No	No	
Ladybird	6	Yes	Yes	Yes	
snail	0	Yes	Yes	No	
Worm	0	No	No	No	
Wood louse	30	Yes	Yes	No	

These are two of the records

Figure 7.5 An animal database

The different database programs then offer you ways of searching for the information. Questions like 'What animals have six legs and no wings?' will give you a list of animals with those properties. More sophisticated search devices will accept questions such as 'What animals have six legs, no wings and a shell?' and will give you a much smaller list and an answer closer to the question you really wanted to ask.

Using the encyclopedia with children – 'Where do I live?'

The outcomes for this lesson are that the children will learn that CD-ROMs hold large amounts of information and recognise the need for search tools. Check that the CD-ROM is already installed and whether you need the actual CD-ROM to run the program. Make sure that before the session you have accessed it and are fully aware on how to search for information. Ensure you know about the capability of CD-ROMs to store lots of information (all the content in most school libraries can be contained within two CD-ROMs). Ask the children about their question:

- What are they trying to find?
- How many different ways are there of finding the answer?
- What words are they are going to type in the search box?
- What animal names are in their question?

Using this information, search the encyclopaedia using the key words in the question and see what results you get. As searching requires the word to be spelt accurately you could deliberately misspell the word and see what happens. Most encyclopaedias can be quite difficult to read but the *Eyewitness Children's Encyclopedia* has a friendly voice-over facility which reads the text. Although this can be used with the children, you should also read the answer to the children.

After first trying with the key words, use the menus to see if you get any different answers to your search. It may be that the information you get from your search is exactly what you wanted in which case you will want to save it. Press the **Copy** button on the screen to save the information to the clipboard of the computer from where you can paste it into another document such as the word processor. There is more information on using the clipboard in Chapter 8, *Using ICT to Support Art and Design*.

Activity 7.4
Using ICT to develop questions and answers

The title may seem a little complicated, but have no fear as there is a particular type of software that may help you or the children find answers and help in the formulation of questions. In science there is often a need to identify things such as rocks, animals, plants, materials, etc. In any identification procedure there are ways of identifying particular things by certain key features. For example, we know that a 50p coin is silver in colour, has no serrated edges and has seven sides. These key items of information identify the coin as a 50p and not a 10p coin. For the children, you can think of the important pieces of information that might identify pets. Figure 7.6 provides an example of the possible sequence of questions. In this structure each question has just two possible answers (yes or no) and there are only two branches from each point so the arrangement is called a binary tree (or sometimes a decision tree). There are software programs available that offer children the opportunity to use and create binary trees. A popular program that is suitable for Key Stage 1 is the *Microsoft Decision Tree.*

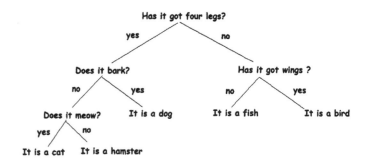

Figure 7.6   A binary tree of children's pets

Using the binary tree with children

The object of this session is to use a prepared file to identify objects and know that the program constructs a binary tree. It is important that the children understand the identification process as this helps in the formulation of relevant questions. To achieve this the teacher may ask you to help in the construction of a paper-based binary tree before using the *Decision Tree* software.

A paper-based binary tree

This uses a set of objects with which the children are familiar such as a set of objects made from different materials. In this exercise we have a metal spoon, wooden spoon, piece of paper, plastic spoon, cork and a stone. Some strips of paper are prepared and two of the objects are selected, e.g. the plastic and metal spoons. The children are asked to suggest a question that will distinguish between them. This could be 'Is it shiny?', 'Is it metal?', 'Is it plastic?' or some other question. Choose the question and write it on the strip of paper. Put two arrows going from the question with the metal spoon at the end of the *Yes* arrow and the plastic spoon at the end of the *No* arrow. Now introduce another object, the wooden spoon. Ask the first question again. This time the answer will be no and the wooden spoon will join the plastic spoon. Now a question has to be asked to distinguish the plastic spoon from the wooden one. 'Is it plastic?', 'Is it heavy?', 'Is it red?' could be one of a variety of questions. Decide upon the question and write it on another slip of paper and add the yes and the no arrows. Place the plastic spoon at the end of the *Yes* arrow and the wooden spoon at the end of the *No* arrow. This process is then repeated with all of the objects and the tree is completed.

In another exercise with a group of Year 1 children the decision tree shown in Figure 7.7 was recorded (Kate Norman, Primary Science Review, Association for Science Education March/April 2000).

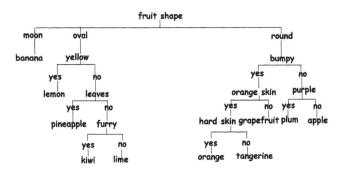

Figure 7.7   A binary fruit tree

Using the computer program

For this exercise to be successful again you should make sure that you have used the program before working with the children. You will probably find a collection of programs linked to the identification of trees, fruit, small animals (minibeasts). In this exercise you will be using the fruit program. Make sure that you are aware of the range of fruits on the program – ideally you want the children to select a fruit that can be identified by the program. In science it is important that the children handle/observe the real objects as much as possible. In this case a collection of different fruits can be brought into the classroom so that the children can feel and smell them. It is likely that the children will know the names of some of the fruits, in which case get them to pretend that they have never seen the fruit before, that it comes from somewhere far away and they want to find out what it is called.

Get the children to select a small fruit and ask them to describe it, without naming it. What are its important features? Talk about the words used to describe it and write them down:

- What colour is it?
- Is it smooth?
- How hard is it?
- Does it have a stone inside it?

Now start the program. Select the file that you want to use and ask the children to read the first question and decide whether a yes or no answer is appropriate.

DfEE/QCA (1999) *The National Curriculum*. London. DfEE.

Further reading

Chapter 8

Using ICT to Support Art and Design

The QCA Scheme of Work for art and design at Key Stage 1 and 2 (QCA 1999a) makes the following statements about the use of ICT. The use of ICT can help children's learning in art and design by:

- providing additional equipment and tools to help them produce and manipulate images and play with ideas and possibilities for the creative use of materials and processes;
- extending the possibilities for recording, exploring and developing ideas for practical work in an electronic sketchbook;
- making it possible for them to document the stages in the development of their ideas electronically, share this with others and review and develop their work further;
- providing a range of information sources to enhance their knowledge and understanding of the work of artists, craftspeople and designers;
- extending the possibilities for sharing their work with others via e-mail or developing a school gallery on a website.

Activity 8.1
Drawing and
painting with the
nursery class
using ICT

Paint programs that are common in the classroom are those such as *Paint it* (JETSoft) and *Paint box*. These are in addition to the *Microsoft Windows* program *Paint* which is sometimes used in the classroom. All of these programs have the same basic set of tools that allow pictures to be created on the screen and it is well worthwhile becoming familiar with some of them. The dotted rectangle and star shown in Figure 8.1 are the **Selection** tools. If you want to move a part of the painting to another area of the screen or **Copy**, **Cut** and **Paste** part of the picture into another piece of work, you first need to select the part of the picture you are going to work on. The **Star** allows you to select an irregular area while the **Rectangle** allows the selection of a rectangular part of the screen. Click on the tool, move the mouse to where you want to start the selection and then, holding the left-hand button of the mouse down, drag the tool over the object you want to select from one corner to the opposite corner (see Fig. 8.2).

selection tools

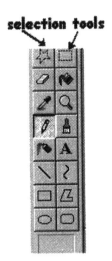

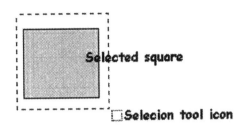

Figure 8.2 A selected square

Figure 8.1 Some tools used in *Paint* programs

The **Rubber** erases that part of the picture that you want to lose while the small bottle with what looks like ink pouring out is a tool called the **Flood Fill** tool. Clicking on this tool and moving it into the drawing area will have dramatic effects, flooding colour onto the screen probably in places where you had no wish for it to go. Don't worry if you make a mistake – there is usually a button that helps you undo the problems. Go to **Edit** on the top bar and click on the **Undo** button. The only time this is unlikely to work is after you have saved your work. Some *Paint* programs have an additional **Undo** button, as do word processing programs, that overrides the top bar.

Other common tools are the **Dropper** which is used to help select paint colours. Click the **Dropper**, move the cursor to a colour, click on it and you will find that this colour then becomes the selected colour. The **Paint Brush** and the **Spray Cans** are used to create the picture along with the line and shape tools. There is usually an option somewhere in the program that allows you to change the size of the brushes or the size of the area affected by the spray can. Some of the children's software paint programs have some interesting extra features. For example, *Paint box* has a set of pre-selected pictures which can be coloured in. *Paint it* has a wonderful stamping and repeating tool which then allows animation of the completed drawing (see Fig. 8.3).

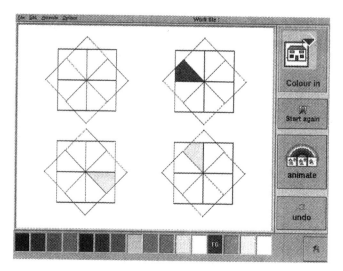

Figure 8.3   The *Paint it* window

The colour printer

This is an essential item for any painting exercise. Colour ink jet printers use four individual colour cartridges – black, cyan, yellow and magenta. These are the primary colours and can be used to create all the other colours e.g. yellow and cyan to make green and magenta and yellow to make red.

My printer is printing the picture in funny colours. This is because one of the colours is running out. It is unlikely that the printer will have an automatic cut-off when an ink cartridge runs out, so it begins to fail to make contributions to the colour mixing. If a green area of the painting is being printed and the yellow runs out, that part of the painting takes on a dramatic cyan hue. First make sure that the picture is saved on the computer. Stop the printer by using the printer controls in the bottom right-hand corner of the screen and replace the empty cartridge (there is no need to switch off the printer). When completed make sure that the printer is on-line (is the indicator light on?) and reprint the picture.

Copying, cutting and pasting

Inevitably at some point the handling of text and pictures will involve cutting and pasting. It is an important skill and the terms used are reminiscent of the actual actions that would be associated with this activity if real paper were being used. The advantage of using a computer is that the original item is not destroyed. First you need to select the item that you want to be copied. In a *Paint* program you use the selection tool, in a word-processing package you would highlight the text by dragging the text cursor over the text with the mouse button held down. Once selected it needs to be copied. This is done by going to the **Edit** button at the top of the screen and clicking on it . In the dropdown box you will see the word **Copy**. Click on this and the selected item is copied to the computer's temporary memory, which is sometimes called the **Clipboard**. You then move to where you want to place the copied item. This could be in a different program, for example you may want to move the picture into a word-processing program. Start the word-processing program and again go to the **Edit** button, and now when you click you will see the word **Paste**. Click on this and the picture that you have copied will appear in the word-processing program.

Some children have difficulty holding down two keys simultaneously. This can be overcome by using the **Sticky Key** option in the **Accessibility Options** in the **Control Panel** of the computer. The sticky key option allows the user to press a key, like the **Shift** key, once and it will 'stick'.

Using a *Paint* program with children – painting a picture

The outcomes linked to this activity are that the children will be able to choose colours from a menu; use the flood fill tool; talk about different colours. In this exercise you are asked to work with the children to paint a picture on the computer using the computer program *Paint it*. Part of this program presents the children with a series of pictures that they can paint in various colours using the flood fill tool. These are called templates (a template is shown in Fig. 8.3). This will lead them through the process of selecting and deleting different colours. After the picture has been painted it can be printed, stuck onto card and with some astute scissors work made into a jigsaw.

Start the program and select a picture. Talk about the picture with the children:

- What is it?
- What colour would they be?
- Look at the colour palette and talk to them about the names of the colours.
- What colour shall we choose?

Show the children how to select the colours and let them take it in turns to select and colour in various sections of the painting. After the picture has been completed, ask them what they think of the colours and again talk about the names of the colours. Tell them about printing the pictures and show them what to do. Ask one child to click on the **Print** button.

When the painting is printed compare it to the picture on the screen. Do they notice any differences in the colours? Are they lighter, darker or very different? This will be an opportunity to use different words to describe the colours, not to describe why the two are different. As an additional activity the children could glue the pictures to a thin piece of card and cut it into eight pieces. This jigsaw can then be put together by other children.

Activity 8.2 Painting in the style of an established painter using the WWW

The WWW has been used extensively by painters as a repository of catalogues of their work, and museums and art galleries throughout the world have put copies of the famous paintings they hold onto the WWW. Popular paintings that are used to provide stimulus to children are paintings such as *Yellow Islands* by Jackson Pollock. Work by artists such as Guiseppe Archimoldo, L. S. Lowry, Paul Klee and Piet Mondrain are also regularly used as stimuli. *Yellow Islands* is in the Tate Gallery and is indexed on the WWW as http://www.tate.org.uk/servlet/WorkImage?id=17411 at the time of writing. Go to http://www. europosters.com/arcimbol.htm for Guiseppe Archimoldo paintings. For L. S. Lowry the Tate Gallery is an excellent source of examples with at least four paintings on view. Go to the Tate Gallery home page at http://www.tat.org.uk and search the collections. For Paul Klee and Piet Mondrain try searching the WWW using one of the search engines.

Searching the WWW

The WWW is searched using a search engine like *Infoseek* which has http://www.infoseek.go.com as its URL (Universal Resource Locator or address). Type this into the address box at the top of the browser after deleting the address that is already there. You will find that it is not necessary to type in the http:// part of the address as the browser will automatically add this for you.

Once at the search engine type in Paul Klee in the search box and either click on the **Search** button or press the **Enter** button on your keyboard. The search engine works by looking through all its entries in its database that include the word 'Paul' and the word 'Klee'. This finds in the region of 1500 articles linked to Paul and Klee. It is possible with some search engines like *Infoseek* to choose to search and display just pictures.

Working with children

The outcomes expected for this activity are that most children will use a computer graphics package to create a picture by selecting the most appropriate tools to match their purposes. If they have not made so much progress they will use a computer graphics package to create a picture. When they have progressed further they will use a computer graphics package to create a picture; select the most appropriate tools to match their purposes; develop an image and modify and correct their work as they go (QCA Scheme of Work for ICT 2B, QCA 1999b).

In this work the teacher has shown the children the painting *Yellow Islands* by Jackson Pollock and has discussed with the children the rhythmic pattern created by the flow of black lines. Your task is to work with the children using the drawing package to create a picture in the form of Jackson Pollock. To help the children with the icons in the drawing program it is sometimes useful to produce flash cards to show to the children to remind them of the meaning of the different icons. Children can find mouse controls difficult so you might want to change the speed of movement of the mouse pointer. This can be achieved by accessing the **Control Panel**.

Creating pictures in the style of Paul Klee is an activity that is particularly suitable for children who are less confident in using the mouse. Talk to the children about what they are doing:

- Are they using thick or thin lines?
- What colours are they using?
- Are the lines short or long?
- What shape is that?

QCA (1999a) *Scheme of Work: Primary Art and Design.* London: DfEE.
QCA (1999b) *Scheme of Work: Information and Communications Technology.* London: DfEE

Further reading

Chapter 9

Using ICT to Support Special Educational Needs

Every learner has an entitlement to all elements of learning. For learners with Special Educational Needs (SEN), the use of ICT can convert this entitlement into reality by providing:

- physical access to the teaching and learning environment;
- access to areas of learning which were previously unobtainable;
- support in the form of tools which lead to independent learning.

The National Curriculum makes it clear that each area of the curriculum should support this process. The Code of Practice, published by the DfE (1994), identifies seven categories of learning difficulty or disability:

1. learning difficulties
2. visual impairments
3. specific learning difficulties
4. emotional and behavioural difficulties
5. hearing impairments
6. physical disabilities
7. speech and language difficulties

It is unlikely that you will be working with children with severe difficulties, but you may be asked to support other people like the Special Educational Needs Coordinator (SENCO) in a variety of ways. This section therefore gives an overview of the types of ICT support that is available for children with special needs. Where ICT offers special provision linked to particular activities these are included within the curriculum areas of this book.

Physical access – looking at the equipment

The computer

A computer can be adapted in a variety of ways for a learner with special needs. In particular the *Microsoft Windows* software is designed to allow adaptation of the interface between the computer and the learner where it is deemed necessary. There was a time when changes to the access of the computer would have had dramatic effects upon its performance. Luckily this is no longer the case and the *Windows 98* software has an accessibility option which is available through the **Control Panel** and is described later in this chapter. There are also other accessibility options linked to the input and output systems of the computer.

Helping the input – the keyboard

The keyboard can have many adaptations to make it easier for the users. Some learners find it easier to use lower case letters on keys and stickers are available to accommodate this. Water, sand, chalk and other liquids often precipitate possible problems with the keyboard. A simple solution is to cover the keyboard with Clingfilm. This is particularly important if a laptop is being used as spillage on a laptop keyboard can be disastrous.

The positioning of the keyboard can be crucial for some learners. Seating and positioning, combined with a well placed keyboard, can make all the difference between writing and concentrating on staying upright. In addition to the traditional keyboard there is always the potential to use the alternative concept or overlay keyboard described in Chapter 5. Overlay keyboards can be very effective replacements for the standard keyboard. A personalised overlay can be provided that will suit the needs of the individual child. Overlay keyboards can be used with all the standard computers found in schools providing the computer has an appropriate socket to receive the overlay keyboard cable link.

Helping the input – the mouse

The other major input device for a computer is the mouse. Displacing the keyboard as the major input device for feeding data into the computer, the mouse can however be a barrier for some learners. A mouse is a device that has to be moved across a surface so that the pointer (cursor) on the screen can imitate the movement. When the cursor, and the mouse, reaches a particular point on the screen a button on the mouse has to be pressed, either once or twice quickly. Alternatively the mouse button has to be held down while the mouse and the on-screen cursor continue their movement. This might be an easy task for some children, but for those with special needs this very complex set of actions can be almost an impossibility. To aggravate the situation some computers, like the Macintosh, have a one-button mouse, some have two and some, like the older Acorn computers and some PCs, have three buttons.

However difficult it might seem, some children with learning difficulties manage to cope with the traditional mouse with no problems. For those with problems there are some good alternatives such as tracker balls and switches. The tracker ball is an upside-down mouse that controls the on-screen cursor. As it is much larger than a normal mouse, children with difficulties in fine motor control have far more control than they would do otherwise (see Fig. 9.1). In addition to the larger ball, tracker balls are provided with large clearly visible buttons.

Figure 9.1   A tracker ball

If control of the mouse is an unobtainable objective the children could use switches. Switches are substantial items that allow pressure to be applied in a variety of directions (see Fig. 9.2). The application of the pressure on the switch is linked to the movement of the cursor on the screen, which in turn results in the ability to navigate around the computer program. Invariably the attachment of switches to a computer needs the installation of specialist software, so the switch option will have to be set up by the class teacher or IT Coordinator.

Figure 9.2   A switch

Helping the output – the monitor

The monitor and printer are the main output devices. With the more modern computers, the monitor is both the visual and audio output device, very much like a television. The way in which the monitor's visual properties can be changed was discussed in Chapter 2. Using the **Control Panel** and the **Accessibility** areas of the computer it is possible to change contrast and font size. Printing from a computer is important. There is no point engaging the children in a word-processing exercise if the work is not subsequently printed out. A learner with difficulties may have been working with pictures or symbols on a computer and a printout of these activities, in particular the images, will provide a stimulus for further work.

Using ICT with children with Special Educational Needs

As a teaching assistant you will find that there are a variety of roles in which you can support the learner with educational needs. For children with reading problems, the reading of ICT text can be accompanied by tracking the text by highlighting it as the words are spoken. Computers can record voices and other sounds. The teacher or assistant could provide voice-over for existing text.

The spell checker has proved an invaluable aid to children with specific learning difficulties like dyslexia and it is always worth finding out how such a device is set up on the computers you will be using. For the *Microsoft Word* program look in **Tools** and click on **Spelling and Grammar** before going to **Options** at the bottom of the dialog box. This box will indicate the options that are available for use.

Further reading

DfE (1994) *Code of Practice on the Identification and Assessment of Special Educational Needs*. London: Central Office of Information.

Chapter 10

Using ICT to Support Your Own Work

File management on your computer

To many that are new to computers this is one of the most daunting areas, perhaps because it challenges our concept of tidiness. Used effectively, the file management system on a computer is exactly the same as being tidy with your bits of paper in the home or at work.

As you may have spent so many tense hours working on the computer in the early stages of your ICT experience, it is worthwhile saving your work. This is where the problem starts. The first time you click on **File** and then **Save**, or you click on the floppy disk icon in the tool bar, a dialog box appears asking a lot of questions. The messy dialog box shown in Figure 10.1 is the one linked to the authors' computer. What would you do if faced with this? Before moving on to that stage, you should know something about how you can organise a filing system within a computer.

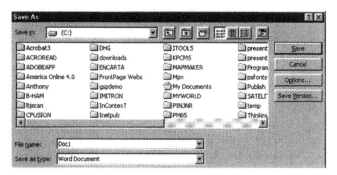

Figure 10.1   The **Save As** dialog box

Folders

Each disk drive on a computer can be treated like a drawer in a filing cabinet. Inside the drawer of a filing cabinet you have a number of folders where you keep your files of work. On a computer disk drive is the drawer and you can divide the space on the disk up into a number of separate areas called folders (see Fig.10.1a). Figure 10.1

shows the folders in the **C** drive (hard disk) of a computer. Each of the folders has been given a name, and in each of those folders are files that are relevant to that area of work. It probably differs from your filing cabinet in that within each folder there could be subfolders and even within each subfolder there could be more subfolders which finally hold the files of work.

Figure 10.1a **Folder** icon

On your computer you are likely to find a folder called **My Documents** (look for it in Figure 10.1). This is a folder especially created by *Microsoft Windows* to help you with the file storage problem. Double clicking on this folder in the authors' computer brings up yet another dialog box which shows the subfolders that are in the **My Documents** folder (see Fig. 10.2). If you double clicked on **Presentations** you would get another set of subfolders that are in the **Presentations** folder. Notice however that in the **My Documents** area there are some files in addition to the folders. For example the *BHAMHIST* file and the *Indexing exercise* file. These have different icons to the folders and if you moved the mouse cursor over them and double clicked, the *Microsoft Word* program would start, and the text in the file would appear on the screen. These files could be described as the ones that got away – they are the equivalent of loose pieces of paper on the desk waiting to be tidied away in a folder.

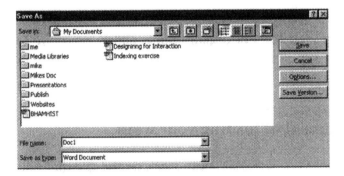

Figure 10.2 Inside the **My Documents** folder

Creating a folder and saving your work

This is straightforward. Click on the **New Folder** icon: a new folder prompt will appear on the screen and the text **New Folder** is highlighted (see Fig. 10.3). Move the mouse cursor to the highlighted area, click on it and type the name of the new folder in the box. Click **OK** and the new folder should appear along with the other folders in the **My Documents** area.

Figure 10.3   The **New Folder**

To save your work, double click on the folder that you have just created and all the other subfolders in the window disappear. You have now opened your folder and as there are no files in it, it is an empty folder. You will find that the piece of work that you are attempting to save already has a name given to it by your computer. This will be something like **Doc1** or **Doc2**. In Figure 10.2 it is called **Doc1**. It is important for your own sanity that you give the file a name that will help you find it later. This is not a problem when you have only one or two files, but when you have more than ten you will find you need a naming system and to have all your files labelled as **Doc** files will make life difficult. Move the mouse to the **File name** box and double click on the **Doc** word to highlight it and then start typing your file name. The highlighted text will disappear immediately you start typing and be replaced by your text. When you have finished click **OK**. You now know that your file is saved on the **C** drive in the folder **My Documents** and in that folder there is another folder created by you in which your file is stored. If you want to save your file in a folder on a floppy disk then you start the procedure outlined above by clicking on the small downward arrow on the right-hand side of the **Save in** box . This shows all the drives on your computer. Select **A** (make sure you have a floppy disk in the **A** drive) and then go through a similar procedure.

Depending upon your level of organisational ability, or desire to be organised, you can create a filing system with any level of complexity.

Opening a document or loading your work

Supposing you wanted to do some more work on the file that you have saved on the **A** drive. How do you find it? Firstly you have to open the program that you would like to use, in this case the word-processing program. Go to **File** on the top bar, click and choose **Open**. It is likely that the dialog box that opens will be set to display the files that are in the **My Documents** folder. If this is the case, you will first have to open the **A** drive by going to the **Open in** box, clicking on the downward arrow and selecting the **A** drive by clicking on it. You will then find the **A** drive folder arrangement and move through these folders until you find the file that you want (see Fig. 10.4).

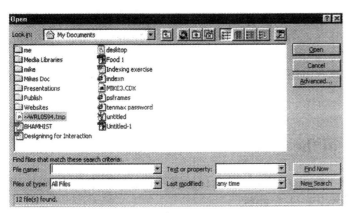

Figure 10.4   Opening a document

The schedule

You will find that in this exercise we are only using a small part of the word processor's capabilities. This section intends only to take you through a few of the word-processor's functions so that you will gain confidence in its use and perhaps produce something that you can use with your teacher in the classroom.

An observation schedule should help you look at what the children are doing in a more meaningful way. We all spend time looking at what other people are doing, and although it is sometimes interesting it is rarely informative. An observation schedule helps the observations to become more focused. To create your schedule you will need to have a clear idea of what the outcomes of the lesson are. In this instance we will imagine that you are working with some children to create some labels. The outcomes are that the children will have typed their name; changed the font and centred it in the page; saved the file and printed it. Your work with the children will give you an opportunity to discover how difficult they find the processes that lead to these outcomes. Observing children is not easy, so the assumption is that you will only be able to closely observe and make notes on one child.

The observation schedule will therefore have the following information:

- Name
- Class
- Date

It will then have questions relating to the outcomes which in this instance will be:

- Could use the keyboard to type name.
- Could correct mistakes (delete letters).
- Could highlight the text.
- Could centre text in middle of page.
- Could choose font size and change size of text.
- Could save and print text.

Using a word processor to create an observation schedule

All of these will have a 1, 2, 3 number associated with them which you will be able to circle when you have observed the children enough to make a decision. For example, 1 would mean 'Only possible with lots of help from the teacher' while 3 would be 'Can do it with no help'.

The creation of the observation schedule

When you start *Microsoft Word* the top of the screen (Fig.10.5) will contain the following elements:

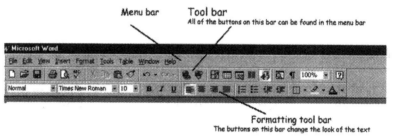

Figure 10.5 The *Microsoft Word* tool bar

Open a new document by clicking on **File** then **New** (Fig. 10.6) or click on the **New** icon on the tool bar (Fig. 10.7).

Figure 10.6 **New** from **File**   **Figure 10.7 New** document icon

Slide the mouse arrow onto the new page that has appeared (note the flashing black cursor on the page). Start typing the following (Fig. 10.8):

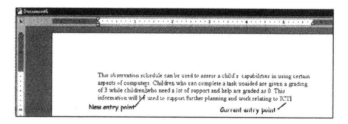

Figure 10.8 Beginning to type

When you have reached the end move the mouse to the new position, click once and the flashing black cursor will take up the new position. As already mentioned, when you reach the end of the line the cursor automatically moves to the next line (word wrapping). If you wish to deliberately create a new line you will need to press the **Return** or **Enter** key on your keyboard. To remove unwanted lines or spaces, press the back space **(BkSp)** key or the delete **(Del)** key.

You will now need to save your work (dealt with in detail earlier in this chapter). Click on the disk symbol on the tool bar. Find the **My Documents** folder in the **Save in** box and create a new subfolder in the **My Documents** folder. Give your file the **File name** *Observation* and click on **Save** (see Fig. 10.9). Now move the text cursor to the beginning of your typing and click on the **Enter/Return** button twice. The whole block of text should move downwards. Move the text cursor to where the text originally started and click the mouse button so that the flashing cursor moves to this position. Type 'Observation Schedule' then press the **Enter/Return** twice. Type 'Name' and then press the **Tab** button four times. The tab button is on the left-hand side of the keyboard (see Fig. 10.10).

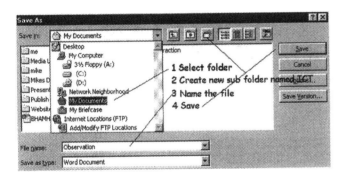

Figure 10.9 The **Save As** dialog box

Figure 10.10 The **Tab** button

After typing 'Name' press the tab button four times and type 'Class'. Repeat this to type 'Date'. You should have the screen shown in Figure 10.11.

Move the text cursor down to the end of the statement and click. Then press Enter/Return twice. Type into the next line 'Could use keyboard to type name'. Then press the Tab button five times, type

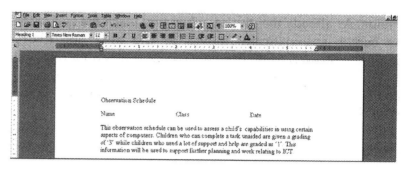

Figure 10.11 The observation schedule

'1', press the Tab twice and type '2' and again twice and type '3'. After typing '3' press Return twice (this means there is a space between the two lines of text) and type in the next statement 'Could correct mistakes (delete letters)'. This time press the Tab button only twice and you should be able to type the '1' exactly under the original '1' in the first row. Continue until the schedule is finished. Adjust the number of times you press the Tab so that the numbers line up neatly under each other (see Fig. 10.12).

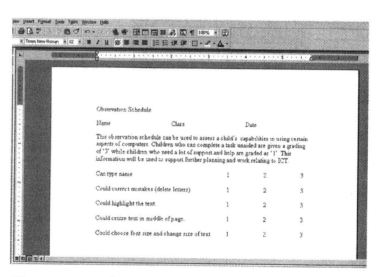

Figure 10.12 The final schedule

The final observation schedule can now have a little bit of gloss added. To make the title text bigger and bolder you will need to highlight the text you want to work on. Move the text cursor to the beginning of 'Observation Schedule'. Click once and then holding the mouse button down drag the text cursor over the two words. This highlights them and allows you to perform the task of font size change and moving the text to the centre of the page (see Fig. 10.13). The final schedule can now be printed.

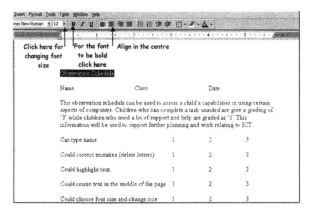

Figure 10.13   Adding gloss

This exercise could be completed using a database program such as *Microsoft Access*, however it is a very sophisticated software program that you will probably never use again. An alternative strategy is to use a database program called *Pinpoint* (Blackcat Software). This is a powerful database program that is intended for use at Key Stage 2.

Analysing the access that children have to computers

What is a database program?

A database program helps you collect different types of information and to analyse and report on it. *Pinpoint* is divided into four parts:

1. The 'Form Designer' which helps you design the form on which the data is collected.
2. The 'Answer Sheets' which allow the data to be entered into the database.
3. The 'Worksheet' that presents the collected data in table format.
4. The 'Report' which will be the graph or written statement that is presented as a result of questions being asked of the data.

The headings under which the data are collected are called 'fields'.

The question and the information

The first task is to decide upon the questions that we want to answer. This will determine the information that we collect. In this instance we want to see if gender has anything to do with whether the children have access to ICT at home. Does their gender affect this access? The first task is to complete the table that we need to use to collect the data. The fields for the table, with their abbreviations will be:

*   Is the child a boy or girl? (gender)
*   Is there a computer at home? (home computer)

- Does the child have his/her own computer? (own computer)
- Does the child have a sister? (sister)
- Does the child have a brother? (brother)

Creating the table

Open up the *Pinpoint* program by either clicking on the icon in the starting window or going to the **Start** button and moving the mouse up to **Programs**. Select the *Pinpoint* program and double click to start it. When the starting window appears move the mouse to **File** (top right-hand corner), click once, and move the mouse down to **New** click again and the *Pinpoint* window appears (see Figure 10.14). Click on the **question mark** button. Move the mouse to a position in the main window and click the left-hand mouse button. A dialog box appears that asks you some details about the question that you are going to ask (see Figure 10.15).

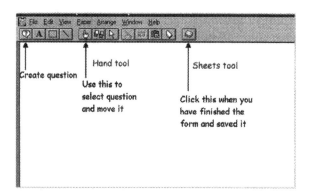

Figure 10.14 *Pinpoint* window

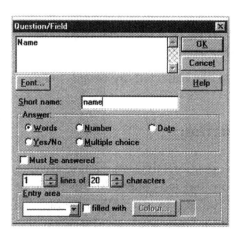

Figure 10.15 Question dialog box

The first question is to ask for the person's name. Type 'Name' in the **Field** box and 'Name' in the **Short name** box. Click on **OK**. This creates a question on the form. The next field of information is the child's gender. Move the question mark icon to somewhere else on the screen and click the left-hand mouse button. The question dialog box appears. Type 'Gender' in the **Field** box and 'Gender' in the **Short name** box. We know that there are only two possible answers so click on **Multiple choice** in the answer area of the dialog box. At this point a smaller dialog box appears that asks you what you want in the multiple choice area. Click on **Add** and type in 'boy' then repeat for 'girl' and click OK (see Fig. 10.16).

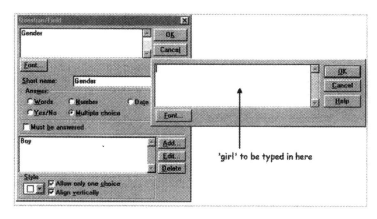

Figure 10.16   Multiple choice questions

Continue for the rest of the questions. In most cases the **Yes/No** answer box will be the type of answer that is required. When you have finished, the questions can be moved around the page using the selection tool (the hand button). If you want to change a question select the arrow and double click on it. The final sheet should look a little like Figure 10.17.

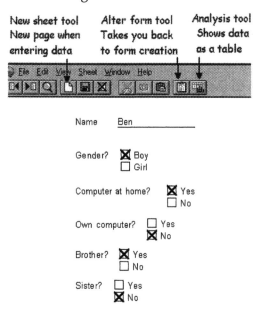

Figure 10.17   The questions

Save the form and click on the **Sheets** tool (see Fig. 10.14). The tool bar at the top changes and the questions are shown in a different environment. This is the 'answer sheet' area of the database program. In this area you can add the data that you have collected from the children. Fill in the boxes and when completed click on the **New Page** icon (Fig. 10.17). This asks you if you want to save the submitted data. Save the data and complete the new form with the data from another child. Continue this process until you have entered all your data. Click on the **Analysis** tool (Fig. 10.17) and a table of your entered data appears (see Fig. 10.18).

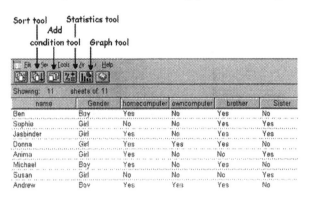

Figure 10.18   The table of data

Analysing the data

At this point in the exercise the data can be analysed to see if the question can be answered. For the question in this exercise, graphs are not really appropriate because all the data is in the form of text (boy, girl, yes, no etc.). Graphical interpretation using the **Analysis** tool is only useful when the data is numerical. The useful tool in this exercise is the **Add Conditions** tool. This tool can be used to look at the table data and isolate the data that is important for the question. Clicking on this tool allows you to look at all the entries that have the following conditions attached to them:

- they are boys;
- they have a computer at home;
- they have no sisters.

This gives a list of all boys who come from an all-boy family and have access to a computer. This list can then be compared to that of one where the girls with access to a computer come from an all-girl family.

Glossary

Analogue This is the way in which electrical signals are used to travel down phone lines. It describes the wave motion of the signals. Now signals are digital – broken up into little bits.

Application This is sometimes the name given to software which performs a useful task, e.g. word processing, spreadsheet and database software.

Backup This is a copy of the work you might be doing stored in a safe place. Computers are trustworthy, but things can happen!

BECTA This is the organisation that has replaced NCET (National Council for Educational Technology). The new name for this organisation is **British Educational Communications and Technology Agency** (BECTA). The agency has a responsibility for the NGfL (National Grid for Learning) which is the WWW site for the government initiative to get all schools on-line and teachers and pupils using it.

Bit Name given to a binary digit. A binary digit is either 1 or 0. A number of bits are strung together to make a byte.

Boolean operator Named after the logician George Boole. Boolean operators are used in search engines and are variables which can either have a value of true or false. They are AND, OR, NOT and you can include them in your search phrases. For example, instead of expressing a wish to find out about 'the planets' you would state 'planets NOT music'.

Browser This is the common name for a World Wide Web (WWW) client. It is a program which sits in your computer (the client computer) and navigates through the World Wide Web and displays pages. The Web browser requests a page from a World Wide Web server based on its Internet address. It retrieves the document from the server and displays the contents on your screen. Common browsers are *Microsoft Internet Explorer* (now in version 4) and *Netscape Communicator*. As World Wide Web pages are written in HTML, browsers are readers of the HTML language.

Bulletin board Bulletin boards, also called newsgroups or discussion groups, work in a similar way to electronic mail. Instead of writing messages to individual users, participants in bulletin boards post their messages on news server. The messages are stored on the news server in hierarchical directories. Users participate in bulletin boards by reading the messages and responding to them. There are bulletin boards or newsgroups on virtually every subject you can think of.

Cache This is part of the computer's memory that is used for temporary storage. When the computer visits the WWW it stores the pages in the cache. This means that when you ask for those pages again it can show them much more quickly.

CD-ROM Compact Disc-Read Only Memory This is now the storage medium for most software programs.

Central Processing Unit (CPU) This is the part of the computer that carries out the processing of information. It sits in the base unit.

Click Depress the left mouse button once and release immediately.

Clipboard This is a temporary memory area of the computer. You can save things in this area and then close the program you are working with. Open another and using the **Paste** button in the **Edit** area of the program, copy the item into that program. If you copy a new item it replaces that already on the clipboard.

Concept keyboard *See* **Overlay keyboard**

Cursor This used to be a very fine line used to pinpoint numbers on something called a slide rule. It is now the mark on the screen made by the mouse. It is normally a small vertical arrow but can take on a variety of shapes.

Data This means 'specific information'. It is a term used to cover both numerical and text information.

Database This is a store of information which has a clear structure. It is basically a huge table with fields along the top and records down the side.

Desktop This is the on-screen display that acts as the backdrop for your applications. It is usually the screen that appears when you start the computer.

Dialog box This is the way in which the computer has a dialogue with you. It displays options for actions.

Directory This is a place on your disk, hard or floppy, where files are stored. Directories are often called folders.

Document A piece of work that has been saved.

Double click Depress the left-hand mouse button twice without a pause.

Download This is the process of transferring files from the server to your computer. The files (they could be programs) are transferred to your computer via the telephone line. They are usually in a compressed form (zipped) and need to be uncompressed (unzipped) before they can be used.

Drag This is the process of moving the mouse with the left-hand mouse button held down.

Email Electronic mail, sometimes also written as E-mail or e-mail. This is the way in which messages are passed from one computer user to another using a local network or by using modems over telephone lines. The message is eventually delivered to the recipient's mailbox which is a file on his/her computer and it can then be read using a mail program such as *Eudora* or *Microsoft Mail*.

Enter key This is a key which is used to tell the computer that you have finished entering a command. In word processing, clicking on the **Enter** key causes the cursor to move down to the next line.

Fields The name given to a category of information. For a database of information on the children in a class the fields could be name; age; eye colour; address; postcode.

File A piece of information, e.g. a document, that is stored in such a way that the computer can access it.

File name The name given to a file.

Floppy disk A removable disk which is used for the storage of computer information. Has a limited capacity.

Folder A section of the disk which is used for storing files.

GIF Sometimes written as Gif or gif, it is an acronym for Graphics Interchange Format, and represents a standard for images, defined in 1987 by Compuserve (a service provider). GIF is a method for encoding compressed pictures that contain up to 8 bits of colour. GIF is not a good way of storing photographic images but is very suitable for pictures or images with large areas of the same colour. Pictures on the Internet are in either GIF or JPEG format.

Graphical interfaces These are the computer-generated screens that you interact with when you switch on the computer and when you move from one program to another in the computer.

Graphical User Interface (GUI) A pictorial screen that acts as the interface through which the user can communicate with the computer.

Hardware A generic term for the 'hard' and tangible parts of your computer. Everything that is not software or is not consumable.

Hyperlink Also referred to as hypertext, this is a term first used by Ted Nelson around 1965 for a collection of documents containing cross-references or 'links' which, with the aid of an interactive browser allow the reader to move from document A to document B simply by clicking within document A or any highlighted reference to document B. The highlighted areas are usually underlined or a different colour or when the mouse arrow changes to a hand. The links are called hyperlinks.

Hypertext Mark–up Language (HTML) This is the programming language that is used to create WWW pages.

Icon A small picture that gives a shortcut to a program or part of a program.

Input The trigger that starts a task, or helps the task continue. Usually made by the keyboard or mouse.

Interface This is something that sits between two things and allows them to interact. *Windows* is an interface. It sits between you and the computer and allows you to do things with the computer that you would not normally be able to do.

Internet This is the collective noun for a large group of networks permanently linked together. Generally it refers to the physical network that makes up the World Wide Web.

Intranet This is the word used to describe an internal network of computers. Your school probably has an Intranet which is connected to the Internet.

ISDN A technical name for an ordinary copper wire that has digital rather than analogue signals running through it.

Joint Photographic Export Group (JPEG) A graphical file format used to display high resolution colour images on the WWW. JPEG images apply a compression scheme that can significantly reduce the large file sizes usually associated with photo-realistic colour images. JPEG compression is not very good for drawn images such as line drawings.

Logo This is a programming language, developed by Seymour Papert, in which sequences of instructions can be given to produce movement in a robot known as a turtle or roamer.

Memory In a computer memory is made up of two types: ROM (Read Only Memory) and RAM (Random Access Memory). This latter memory is the temporary storage space used by the software applications when they are involved in processing information.

Menu bar The bar across the top of the screen which contains clickable options for actions. Items which are displayed in grey are not available.

Modem An electronic device for converting data as used by a computer to data as used by a telephone line. It converts digital signals to analogue signals and vice versa.

Monitor The computer screen or display.

National Council for Educational Technology (NCET) *See* **BECTA**

The National Grid for Learning (NGfL) A must for your favourites button as it will shortly contain lesson notes, plans and pupils' resources that will make the Literacy Hour, the Numeracy 40 min etc. all that more bearable. It contains the Virtual Teachers Centre (VTC), Governor Centre, Standards and Effectiveness Database.

Network Two or more computers linked together to share access to data, information and resources.

Off-line Not connected to the Internet.

On-line Connected to the Internet.

Overlay keyboard A piece of hardware that can be used in addition to a normal keyboard. It is a flat board with a pressure-sensitive skin.

Paste Insert previously cut or copied text or objects.

Peripheral Normally used to refer to any piece of hardware which it attached to or driven by a computer.
Port A socket in the back of the computer into which a peripheral such as a scanner can be connected.

Program A complete set of instructions written in computer language that instructs the processor of the computer what to do and how to deal with a particular solution.

Random Access Memory (RAM) This is the computer's active memory area. In this area all the processing is carried out.

Records The collection of fields relating to a particular item. The item in a collection of information about a class of children could be the information in the fields about the child called Jasbinder.

Right click Press the right mouse button once and release immediately.

Roamer A mobile programmable robot.

Scroll bars The vertical and horizontal strips at the edge of windows on WWW pages. Clicking on them 'scrolls' the window either vertically or horizontally. You can liken it to a 'Dead Sea' scroll that you unwind and read.

Search engines and **search tools** Search engines and search tools are databases which you can use to search for information by typing in key search words into a specially designed form. Your search term is compared against the database contents and a summary of matches or hits is returned to you. Different search engines have different databases so it is worth trying more than one. *Yahoo, Excite, AltaVista, Infoseek, AOLfind* are all examples of search engines.

Server A server is a computer that sits at the centre of a network and usually stores all of the programs that the other computers use. It may be the computer through which the network is connected to the Internet.

Service provider ISP stands for Internet Service Provider while IAP means Internet Access Provider. Both mean a company that provides access to the Internet through its computer. IAPs tend to provide a basic link while ISPs provide additional services. For a sum of approximately £10 per month users who have computers that are not on the Internet can link them to the Internet by connecting them by modem and phone line to the ISP/IAP company computer usually for the cost of a local telephone call.

Smileys : -) This is a symbol by which a person can portray a mood when sending emails. There are hundreds of such symbols, from the obvious to the obscure. The example above expresses happiness.

Software This is a term used to describe programs and other applications. It is distinguished from hardware which describes the computer that the software runs on.

Spreadsheet This is an application which consists of cells arranged in table in which data can be placed.

Stand alone A stand-alone computer is one that is set to work on its own and is not part of a network.

Subfolder A folder within a folder.

Task bar The bar usually found at the bottom of the *Microsoft Windows* screen containing the **Start** menu, buttons showing what software applications are open and the notification area.

Tool bar On-screen row of shortcut buttons.

Uniform Resource Indicator (URL) The 'address' of the WWW document. This gives the location of a file on the WWW and also identifies the Internet service, such as FTP or WWW, that will handle the file.
http://www.abc-project.org.uk/pages.htm
http: indicates the protocol
www.abc-project.org.uk is the network location
pages.htm is the file name

Visual Display Unit (VDU) Usually known as the monitor.

WIMP Windows, Icons, Menus and (mouse) Pointers. A *Microsoft Windows* environment where you are presented with icons and menus and use a mouse and pointers to interact with the system.

Window A window is a rectangular area of the screen that displays a program or part of a program. It may be sized so that it fills the whole screen or part of the screen.

WWW The World Wide Web (the 'Web') is a collection of on-line documents housed on Internet servers around the world. Or for those of a more technical disposition, it is the graphical Internet hypertext service that uses the HTTP protocol to retrieve Web pages and other resources from Web servers. Pages on the WWW usually contain hyperlinks to other pages, documents and files.

Index